Praise for *Life's Greatest Lessons*

"In this book a master teacher shares with us the great depth of his wisdom—a comprehensive philosophy of life for all ages."

> —*Sanford N. McDonnell, chairman emeritus,*
> *McDonnell Douglas Corporation*

"One of the most touching and inspirational books I have read in a long time."

> —*Katie Struckel Brogan, editor,* Writer's Digest

"Life is complicated. Having a cornerstone to build our lives on—and give to our kids—is a must. This book is that cornerstone."

> —*John McCormack, founder and CEO, Visible*
> *Changes, and author,* Self-Made in America

"I just wanted to let you know what a profound impact your book is having on my associates and everyone that I have given the book. . . . I have given out thirty-six copies of the book with raves from everyone about how it has effectively assisted them."

> —*Tom Roth, Bio Lab Industries*

"What a great book! . . . As a seventh grade teacher, I found so many things in this book that I would love to share with my students."

> —*Amanda McColaugh*

"Your book was most helpful to me. I gave it to my husband, and together we used it (and still do) to stay motivated, to appreciate all that we have, and to keep on trying. I believe it offers value in the most fundamental ways—spiritually, physically, and mentally. Thanks for writing such a wonderful book."

> —*Kim Dailey*

"This is a great book for kids, teachers, parents, lawyers, grocery store clerks, grandmas, cousins, friends, and anyone else with a pulse. I thank you, Dr. Urban, for sharing your wisdom, guidance, and moral courage. I, for one, am much better for it!"

—*Kristin A. Loughlin, graduate student*

"I just wanted to say right on! to your book. . . . Thanks . . . for such a wonderful book that I'm sure I'll incorporate in my ministry here in the inner city for many days to come."

—*Reverend Edward Hearn, Baptist minister, Chicago*

"Thank you for your inspiring words. I have read your book . . . and it was absolutely brilliant. . . . Today I use your book on a consistent basis with my students."

—*Eric Stambaugh, high school music teacher*

"Thank you for your wonderful book. It has given real depth and substance to our character education program."

—*Ruth Kistler, sixth grade teacher*

"I will always treasure this book as a reference on how to live a complete life. . . . It has opened my eyes to the important values and attributes to have for a happy and successful life. I hope that others have found the joy that I have from this book. I am grateful for your apparent love for teaching others."

—*Rachel Lundrigan, high school senior*

Also by Hal Urban

Positive Words, Powerful Results

HAL URBAN

Life's Greatest Lessons

20 Things That Matter

A FIRESIDE BOOK
Published by Simon & Schuster
New York   London   Toronto   Sydney

FIRESIDE
Rockefeller Center
1230 Avenue of the Americas
New York, NY 10020

This Fireside Edition 2005

FIRESIDE and colophon are registered trademarks
of Simon & Schuster, Inc.

For information regarding special discounts for bulk purchases,
please contact Simon & Schuster Special Sales
at 1-800-456-6798 or business@simonandschuster.com

Designed by Jan Pisciotta

Manufactured in the United States of America
1   3   5   7   9   10   8   6   4   2

The Library of Congress has cataloged the paperback edition as follows:
Urban, Hal.
Life's greatest lessons: 20 things that matter/Hal Urban.—4th ed.,
1st Fireside ed.
p.   cm.
Rev. ed. of: 20 things I want my kids to know.
"A Fireside book."
Includes bibliographical references (p.   ).
1. Conduct of life. I. Urban, Hal, 1940– . 20 things I want my kids to know. II.
Title.
BJ1581.2.U73   2003   158.1—dc21   2002026652

ISBN 0-7432-3782-X (Pbk)
0-7432-7417-2

For Dan, Mark, and Mike,

When you were much younger, we had to live apart for two years. I wrote you a letter each week and told you about how much I loved you and wanted the best for you. I also wrote about things I wanted you to know. Then you came home, and I didn't need to write any more letters.

Now that you're older and we're living apart again, I've written another letter—this book. I wrote it because you're still young and you're still my kids. I still love you and want the best for you. And the things I want you to know are still the same.

Love,
Dad

Life is a succession of lessons which must be lived to be understood.

RALPH WALDO EMERSON

All great truths are simple in final analysis, and easily understood; if they are not, they are not great truths.

NAPOLEON HILL

CONTENTS

Contents

Preface

A Tribute to Some Special Friends

Life's Greatest Lessons has had an extraordinary journey. It's been knocked out a couple of times but is alive and thriving today because of one group of very kind, conscientious, and committed people. These are new friends who've taken the time to share their appreciation for my simple message about old-fashioned goodness. They've also given the book wings by going back many times to buy more copies for family, friends, and colleagues. Nothing spreads a book around more than word-of-mouth endorsements from enthusiastic readers. And nothing inspires an author more than positive feedback. There are simply no words in our language that could adequately express the depth of my gratitude for the letters, cards, e-mails, and phone calls.

The most common question I've been asked by these wonderful people is, "Can I get the book in hardcover?" Until now, the answer was always no. But I've been blessed to work with people at a publishing company who not only listen to their authors but also to their readers. Countless people have requested a hardcover edition for two main reasons: to give as gifts to treasured friends and to be kept on a shelf with other favorite books. The most touching compliment I've ever received about the book was from a man in Michigan who said he wanted to keep it next to his Bible. This special gift edition is for him and for the many others who've been requesting it for several years.

A Brief History of Life's Greatest Lessons

For those of you discovering this book for the first time, it might be helpful to know a little about its history. Its earliest form took shape many years ago as a series of letters I wrote to my sons when they were young children. Several years later the principles contained in those letters were written as a book for young adults and submitted to more than thirty publishers. I was not prepared for the result: more than thirty rejections. Found among this rubble of denial was one small glimmer of hope: a single editor thought I had a good idea but suggested that at least half the content be eliminated and the other half rewritten. After licking my wounds for more than a year, I took a sabbatical from my teaching position and started over. The result was a shorter and more upbeat version, and it was published in 1992 as *20 Things I Want My Kids to Know*.

It did surprisingly well for a book written by a first-time, no-name author. It sold out its first printing, and I anxiously awaited news about how many copies would be printed on the second run. The answer was zero. The book was mysteriously allowed to go out of print, and it again seemed like the end of the road.

Then along came my readers. They encouraged me to keep the message alive, while pointing out that it wasn't a book just for young adults but for people of all ages. I changed the title, made some minor revisions, and published it myself. Within a few years more than eighty thousand copies were sold from my garage, and *Writer's Digest* selected it as Inspirational Book of the Year. That award, and the urging of my readers to give the book greater exposure and distribution, eventually led me to Simon & Schuster. I am deeply grateful to the people I work with there and to my devoted readers for making the book what is today.

A Special Wish

As I travel and speak throughout the United States and in other countries I find whole-hearted agreement on one of my major points—that good character is the bedrock of a good society. In reading this book, I hope you'll become part of a growing movement to return us to a society known for its civility, virtues, and old-fashioned goodness. May you become a powerful partner in passing on the great lessons of life.

Hal Urban

May 2005

If Someone
Gave You This Book

The person who gave you this book cares about you and wants the best for you. That's what friends and family members do. We want to pass on the great lessons that life has taught us. This book contains some of those lessons. It's given to you as a gift along with the hope and prayer that it will help you think about and better understand the real meaning of success. Please accept it in that spirit, and pass it on to others.

This is a book about what's good—in life and in people—especially in you. It's about inner resources you have but might not be using. It's about tapping into your potential for becoming the best person you can be and for enjoying life to the fullest.

That's what the special person who gave you this book wants for you.

A good book is the best of friends, the same today and forever.

MARTIN TUPPER

Introduction

I Wrote This Book for Four Reasons

1. Because We're Never Too Young or Too Old to Learn Life's Greatest Lessons . . . and the Time Is Always Right

I was a teacher for thirty-five years and loved virtually every minute of it. I had the best of all worlds—I taught kids in a public high school, adults in a Jesuit university, and spoke often to children at the elementary- and middle-school levels. I discovered long ago that regardless of age, people are eager to learn when it means understanding life more deeply and living it more fully. The letters and e-mails I receive from young children, teenagers, and adults confirm this on an almost daily basis.

Saint Ignatius Loyola, one of the world's greatest educators, once said that we only learn when we're ready to learn. In my lifetime, I've never experienced a period like the present in which so many people are not only open to learning, but also to re-examining their values and priorities. After enjoying a sustained period of unprecedented technological and economic advancements, our world has been shaken. The "dot-com" phenomenon imploded; the stock market and the economy took a nosedive; the events of September 11, 2001, both grieved us and reminded us of our vulnerability; and the corporate scandals of 2002 further shocked and dismayed us.

As one who's studied and taught history for many years, I know that tough times ultimately bring out the best in us. When people start asking questions about what's really important, they usually find the right answers. I'm pleased and honored that my book is helping the process.

2. Because They Don't Teach "How Life Works" or "What Is Essential" in School

Our schools, for the most part, do a great job. From first grade through graduate school, they offer a multitude of courses which result in increased knowledge and valuable skills. But there's something missing in the curriculum. We don't teach our students about life itself, about how it works or about what's essential. Never has there been a greater need for that.

We need someplace other than the proverbial "school of hard knocks" to acquire the right tools for succeeding in life. We need help in developing the attitudes and skills necessary to establish satisfying relationships, to set and achieve personal goals, and to enjoy feelings of self-worth.

As an educator, I felt this need for many years. But my pleas fell on deaf ears. Administrators were more concerned with test scores and budgets. Helping our students develop into good human beings didn't seem to be the school's responsibility. So I wrote this book to fill a void, to help us and our kids understand what's important, what good character is, and what it means to be successful in life.

3. Because Most of Us Need Help in Discovering How Good We Can Be

A few years ago, while attending a conference, I heard a psychologist say that by the time a person reaches the age of eighteen, he or she has been put down more than a hundred thousand times. I don't know how he came up with that figure, but it wasn't surprising. The truth is: we *do* get put down too much. It starts at an early age, comes from a variety of sources, and continues well into adulthood. In addition, the news media tells us every day what's wrong with the world and its people. This daily barrage of negatives takes its toll. The more frequently we hear something, the more likely we are to believe it.

It's not my purpose to examine *why* this happens, but simply to point out that it's one of the unfortunate truths about life. I wrote this book because I think we need help in focusing on the other side of humanity. I happen to believe that the overwhelming majority of people in the world are law-abiding, loving, and caring. They just don't get any publicity for it. Being good doesn't make the news. I also believe that most of us sell ourselves short. We have good qualities we're unaware of, have inner resources we haven't discovered, and have opportunities we never dreamed of. I hope this book brings out some positives in a world that seems to dwell on negatives. Finding the good in life can be one of our greatest joys.

4. Because Old-fashioned Truth Never Goes out of Style . . . Even with a New Generation

About a year before I wrote the first draft of this book, I gave a talk called "The Real Meaning of Success" to a group of college students. I began by pointing out some of the messages we get bombarded with constantly. I wanted them to know that my message would be quite the opposite. So I started by telling them what I *didn't* have: I had no "secrets" of success, no "magic formula" for complete happiness, no "amazing new techniques" for attaining the American Dream, no "quick and easy" way to become rich and powerful, and no "unique" method for getting everything we want.

Instead, I spoke that day about such time-honored values as respect, kindness, honesty, appreciation, desire, hard work, commitment, and just being a good person. My point was that there's no shortcut, no easy way, and no new method for achieving real success. It still has to be earned.

I was both surprised and pleased that so many of them stayed afterward. One of them said, "You know, you didn't really say anything I hadn't heard before, but you put it together in such a way that it made more sense. You really shed new light on some old truths." Then an elderly faculty member who was standing nearby said, "Thanks. We all need to be reminded about what's really important." Here were a young man just starting college and an older man nearing the end of his career telling me the same thing. Boy, did I love those two! They helped me decide that I *had* to write this book.

About the 20 Things

Why twenty? There's no profound reason. Probably because thirty is too many and nineteen doesn't sound right. Twenty just happened to be a nice round number that fit with what I had to say. I don't claim they're the *only* twenty things we need to know, just that they're some of the most valuable. They're twenty things I wish I'd known when I was younger. It wasn't until I was in my late thirties that I figured out how life works. Maybe these twenty things will help someone else who's still trying to figure it out. Actually, we need to do more than simply understand. To know them is one thing; to apply them is quite another. As an ancient Chinese proverb tells us:

> I hear . . . and I forget
> I see . . . and I remember
> I do . . . and I understand

Life's
Greatest
Lessons

CHAPTER 1

Success Is More Than Making Money

> *Success means doing the best we can with what we have. Success is in the doing, not the getting—in the trying, not the triumph.*
>
> WYNN DAVIS

LIFE'S MOST IMPORTANT DISCOVERY

I was thirty-nine when I first understood what it meant to be successful. What did I do? Become the CEO of a Fortune 500 company? Drive home in my first Mercedes? Win the lottery? Take home the grand prize on *Who Wants to Be a Millionaire?* None of the above. I just made a simple, yet profound, discovery. I discovered how life works and what its essentials are. After years of missing the point, I began to understand what it means to succeed in life and how to go about it. With this discovery came two things that had always eluded me: a sense of inner peace and a feeling of self-worth. And best of all, I began to enjoy life more than ever before.

So what *was* this great discovery? Is there really a formula for becoming successful? I'm convinced that there is. But you won't find it wrapped up in a nice, neat package and advertised on TV. It's not new, it's not a secret, and there's nothing magical about it. Therefore, it won't sell. It's too old, too simple, and too innocent. But it works.

After years of studying history, philosophy, and psychology, I realized that life and success can be reduced to some fundamental principles that have been around for thousands of years. After following several different paths in search of "the good life," I ended up back where I'd started, and with what I now call old-fashioned truths. As Edward Albee says in his play *The Zoo Story,* ". . . sometimes it's necessary to go a long distance out of the way in order to come back a short distance correctly."

Does this book contain the formula? Will you find it within the "20 Things"? I hope so. I honestly believe that if you apply these age-old principles consistently, you'll both understand and experience the true meaning of success. A Swedish proverb tells us that we get old too quick and smart too late. Maybe that doesn't *have* to happen. Maybe my book will help you get smart earlier than I did. And even if you're older, it's never too late to learn. The smartest people in the world are the ones who know how to be happy.

SUCCESS AND MONEY

We can't seem to make up our minds whether money is good or bad. When someone is described as successful, it usually means he or she is wealthy. So it must be good. But they say money can't buy happiness. So it must be bad. Wealthy people contribute billions of dollars each year to worthy causes. So, it's good. But haven't we heard that money is the root of all evil? Now it's bad again. People who aren't rich criticize those who are, but would love to be rich themselves. So, which is it, good or bad?

It's neither. But because we live in a society which so often equates money with success, it needs to be examined. Some of the myths about it need to be clarified, and it needs to be placed in a proper perspective. There are two points I'd like to make about money:

1. Money is not bad

Does it really say in the Bible that money is the root of all evil? No. It says the *love* of money is the root of all evil. That's quite a difference. There's nothing wrong with money. There's nothing wrong with wanting it, and there's nothing wrong with having it, even in large amounts. The keys are how we earn it and what we do with it. Honestly acquired and well spent, money can be a resource for much good. Can it buy happiness? Whoever said that it can't probably didn't have enough. Actually, it'll buy a lot more happiness than poverty will. I think Pearl Bailey best described it when she said, "Honey, I been poor, and I been rich. And let me tell you, rich is better." It probably is better in most cases. There's nothing illegal or immoral about being rich, but it isn't everything.

2. Money isn't all there is to being successful

During the 1980s, we constantly read and heard about how many people were becoming millionaires . . . and how many millionaires were becoming billionaires. Some of the most celebrated among them went to prison. Ivan Boesky, one of the financial wizards of the day, even went so far as to say, "Greed is good." He said it a few months before being indicted by a federal grand jury. He was willing to say in public what many were feeling in private: success and wealth are synonymous.

Now we look back on the quest for wealth in the 1980s as being somewhat mild. That was just a warm-up for the dot-com and stock-market meteors of the 1990s. We learned on an almost daily basis who the new "instant billionaires" were, and countless people were risking their health, relationships, and resources to join the ranks. And all too often, ethics and some of our most cherished values took a backseat to wealth and the accompanying lifestyle.

The corporate scandals, still unfolding as I write—at Enron, Arthur Andersen, Tyco, Xerox, WorldCom, and others—are

ccessful people understand the difference between
isting and living, and always choose the latter. They
t the most out of life because they put the most into
They reap what they sow. And they enjoy life to the
llest.

OUR POTENTIAL FOR REAL SUCCESS

*In our society today, large numbers of . . . people never
fulfill their potentialities. Their environment may not
stimulate such fulfillment, or it may actually stunt
growth. . . . Our strength, creativity, and growth as a
society depend upon our capacity to develop the talents
and potentialities of our people.*

JOHN GARDNER

ept this quote posted in large letters in my classroom for
 years. It served as a reminder for both me and my stu-
that there's more of us to be realized. John Gardner was
ner secretary of Health, Education and Welfare, the
ler of Common Cause, and the author of several books.
rote in *Excellence* that too many of us never fully develop
se of influences in our environment. I agree. We simply
itzed with too many messages that don't have anything
with real success. We're urged to look for the quick fix
 than to look inside at our own resources. If we don't

perfect examples. At Enron, for instance, the company and its
executives were on top of the world. But they were toppled
because of the way they got there. Their empire now lies in
ruins. And because of what *Newsweek* magazine called "executive avarice" and the "greedy, go-for-broke ethos" of the corporate world, thousands of innocent employees and investors
lost their jobs and much of their life savings.

This is what happens when we lose perspective on money.
Life gets distorted. It wasn't just those who went to prison in
the 1980s or went bankrupt in the 1990s and the early 2000s
who lost themselves in the pursuit of the almighty dollar.
Many of those who made large amounts of money legally and
managed to hold on to it were still coming up empty. The
Tom Peters Group conducted extensive interviews with thousands of business executives during this period. Almost half of
them said that despite years spent striving to achieve their
financial goals, their lives seemed "empty and meaningless."
Sixty-eight percent of the senior executives interviewed said
they had neglected their family lives to pursue professional
goals.

These are people who had money, property, power, and
status. Why weren't they happy? Because having those things
is not the same as being successful. They'd lost sight of what
was essential. They got addicted, becoming slaves to big
money and the things that go with it. In the process, they
damaged their own lives as well as the lives of others. Success
is more than making money. To overemphasize its importance is to cheat ourselves out of the other things that make
life so much more interesting, meaningful, and rewarding.

WHAT *DOES* IT MEAN TO BE SUCCESSFUL?

The great philosopher Thomas Carlyle once wrote, "Let each become all that he was created capable of being." I can't think of a better definition of success. Life challenges us every day to develop our capabilities to the fullest. We're successful when we reach for the highest that's within us—when we give the best we have.

The quote at the beginning of this chapter says that success is in the *doing,* not in the *getting.* I can't emphasize that point enough. Life doesn't require us to always come out on top. It asks only that we do our best at each level of experience. This is what successful people *do* in some of the most important areas of life:

- Successful people accept life as it is, with all its difficulties and challenges. They adapt to it rather than complain about it. They accept responsibility for their own lives instead of blaming or making excuses. They say YES to life in spite of its negative elements and make the most of it, no matter what the circumstances.

- Successful people develop and maintain a positive attitude toward life. They look for good in others and in the world, and usually seem to find it. They see life as a series of opportunities and possibilities, and always explore them.

- Successful people build good relationshi[ps] sitive to the needs and feelings of others. [con]siderate and respectful. They have a way [of bringing] out the best in other people.

- Successful people have a sense of directio[n and pur]pose—they know where they're going. Th[ey set goals,] accomplish them, and then set new goals [. They thrive on] and enjoy challenges.

- Successful people have a strong desire to l[earn about] life, the world, and themselves. They see l[earning as a] joy, not a duty. They continually enrich th[eir lives by] learning new things and improving thems[elves. They] are always discovering, always growing.

- Successful people are action-oriented. The[y get things] done because they're not afraid of hard wo[rk. They] don't waste time. They use it in constructi[ve ways.] They don't get into ruts or become bored [because] they're too busy looking for new experienc[es.]

- Successful people maintain high standards [of per]sonal conduct. They know that honesty is [one of the] main ingredients in the character of a goo[d person.] They are consistently truthful in both thei[r private and] public lives.

look, we don't find, and our capabilities remain hidden. We end up seeing limitations instead of possibilities.

But there's a positive side to all of this. Once we're aware of it, we can do something about it. That's why I had another quote posted next to Gardner's:

The good news is that the best season of your life can be ahead of you no matter what your age or circumstances—if you choose to make it so—because 90 percent of your potential is not only untapped and unused, but also undiscovered. That's not just good news, it's incredible news!

TIM HANSEL

Tim Hansel is an adventurer, speaker, author of six books, and a man who daily squeezes everything he can out of life. He's also a former colleague and a dear friend. When we taught a psychology class together several years ago, we constantly urged our students to look inside—to discover what was good about them and to recognize how much potential they had. We encouraged them to *be* more and *do* more. Surprise! They were eighteen years old and had never heard things like that before.

About a year later, I began to issue the same challenge to my students at the University of San Francisco. Most of them were in their thirties and forties, some older. Guess what? They'd never been taught anything about their potential, either. At the end of a great class discussion on it one evening, a forty-seven-year-old woman seemed to sum things up when she said, "You know, you're right. We spend too much of our time just going through the motions. We *don't* seem to realize our potential." But as Tim reminds us in his quote, it's good news that so much of us is still undiscovered. That's one of the main messages in this book. Whether we're young or old, whether we have a ninth-grade education or a Ph.D., we can always learn more about our potential for becoming the persons we were meant to be. If we look inside, we'll find all the resources we need for real success.

To be what we are, and to become what we are capable of becoming, is the only end of life.
ROBERT LOUIS STEVENSON

CHAPTER 2

Life Is Hard . . . and Not Always Fair

> *Life is a series of problems. Do we want to moan about them or solve them?*
>
> M. SCOTT PECK

ONE OF LIFE'S MOST VALUABLE LESSONS

Life doesn't always work the way we'd like it to. If we had our way, it would be easier, consistently fair, and more fun. There'd be no pain and suffering, we wouldn't have to work, and we wouldn't have to die. We'd be happy all the time. Unfortunately, we don't get our way. We get reality instead. But reality is a great teacher. It helps us learn, although often slowly and painfully, some of life's most valuable lessons. One of them is this: *The world will not devote itself to making us happy.*

Whether we like it or not, this is one of life's great truths, one of our first and most valuable lessons in reality. Philosophers have argued for thousands of years as to why life works the way it does, but that's not our concern. Our concern is *how* it works. If we don't understand and accept life as it is, we'll keep wishing for something else and never get it. We'll keep complaining and whining about the way things should be but never will be. This is one of life's most valuable lessons because once we understand that the world won't devote itself to making us happy, we begin to accept that responsibility for ourselves.

Someone asked me, "Are you sure you want to put these negative ideas near the beginning of the book?" I don't see them as negative. They're near the beginning because they're basic truths and because they're so important. If anything, I see them as ultimately positive. Let me give you an example. I wrote this book on a computer. I'm a lot more successful with it now than I was when it was new. That's because I took the time to find out how it works. It wasn't easy (even though the computer is supposed to be "user-friendly"), but the effort, the mistakes, and even the frustration were worth it in the long run. Life is a lot like that—we get more out of it once we understand how it works.

LIFE IS HARD

Have you ever seen the bumper sticker that says, "Life is hard—and then you die"? I laughed the first time I saw it. Then I wondered *why* I was laughing. It must have been the element

of surprise. There was one of the great truths of life staring m
in the face from the rear end of someone else's car. It wa
something I would have expected to read in a book written by
one of the ancient philosophers.

In fact, it *is* one of the ancient philosophers who is usually
credited with saying it first. About 2,500 years ago, Buddha
wrote what became known as the Four Noble Truths. The first
one was "Life is suffering." He may have been the first to write
it, but I suspect that many people had it figured out a long time
before he came along. It would be hard to believe that the
world's earliest inhabitants had it any easier. Life *is* hard. It always has been, and it always will be.

The first three words in psychiatrist M. Scott Peck's highly
acclaimed book *The Road Less Traveled* are "Life is difficult."
Peck calls this one of the greatest truths because once we
understand and accept it, we can live more effectively. Instead
of moaning about our problems, we can look for ways to
solve them. One of the main differences between those who
succeed and those who fail can be found in how they
approach life's difficulties. Failures try either to avoid their
problems or to work around them. Successful people accept
them and work *through* them, even when it includes some
suffering. It's this process of meeting our problems head-on
and looking for solutions that gives life meaning.

The problem with too many people, regardless of age, is
that they either don't understand or don't accept the fact that
life involves a certain amount of hardship. They fight against
it instead of adjusting to it. They grumble and complain,
both to themselves and others, about the magnitude of their

They talk as if their difficulties are unique, and
l that life is easier for everyone else. Complaining
ke problems go away. It only makes them worse,
as a magnifying effect. Complaining is an attempt
ur problems on others, a way of refusing to accept
ecessary conditions of life.

ng ago I ran into a former student who's now in his
. After filling me in on what he had been doing, he
"I'm glad I had you as a teacher." Naturally I was flat-
but I was also curious. I always wonder what my stu-
remember some years after being in one of my classes.
asked why. He said, with a knowing smile on his face,
ecause life is hard." He said that that simple truth had
lped him work through some rough spots in his life since
inishing high school. Then he reminded me of the time
when he first heard it.

When he was a freshman in one of my World Studies
classes, I had given a particularly challenging assignment. I
warned the kids in advance that I was going to make them do
two things teachers weren't supposed to make their students
do: think and work. After a few good-natured groans, they
started in. About halfway through, someone said, "This is
hard." I responded the way I always do: "*Life* is hard." We
then proceeded to have a wonderful discussion about philosophy, life, work, pain, joy, and success. Now, years later, this
former student probably doesn't know the capital of
Malaysia, but he does know that life is hard. More importantly, he has accepted it.

Once we accept the fact that life is hard, we begin to grow. We begin to understand that every problem is also an opportunity. It is then that we dig down and discover what we're made of. We begin to accept the challenges of life. Instead of letting our hardships defeat us, we welcome them as a test of character. We use them as a means of rising to the occasion.

At the same time, we need to understand that society bombards us daily with messages that are quite the opposite. To begin with, technology has provided us with push-button living. We can open the garage door, cook dinner, wash the dishes, record our favorite TV program, and pay our bills by simply pushing the right buttons. In addition, we're told over and over that there's a quick and easy way to do just about everything. Within just the past few days, I've read or heard that you can lose a hundred pounds, learn to speak a foreign language fluently, become a hot new radio personality, get a contractor's license, and make a million dollars in real estate. You can do all of these in a matter of days, and with little or no effort. And pigs can fly.

Those ads are all around us because the people in advertising and marketing have a good understanding of human behavior. They know that most people *don't* accept life as hard and will continue to look for the quick and easy way instead. In the previous chapter, I said that successful people accept life as it is. Part of that is understanding that things worth achieving don't come quickly or easily. They come with a price. They come as the result of time, effort, sacrifice, and pain. Because life is hard.

AND IT'S NOT ALWAYS FAIR

In 1981, Harold Kushner, describing himself as being "hurt by life," wrote a book for others who have been hurt yet deserved something better—that is, if life was always fair. The book is called *When Bad Things Happen to Good People*. It became one of the most widely read books of the 1980s. It's a classic because it deals with one of our oldest and most universal questions: "Why?" Or better yet, "Why me?" Kushner had every reason to ask the question. His son, Aaron, was diagnosed at age three as having progeria—rapid aging disease. He suffered physically, his family suffered emotionally, and he died at fourteen. He and his family both deserved better.

Unfortunately, life *isn't* always fair. It's probably the most painful truth we have to learn and the hardest to accept. Bad things *do* happen to good people—sometimes to others, sometimes to us. And it seems all too often that they happen when least deserved. In addition, we see good things happen to people who don't deserve that, either. As it says in the Bible, the sun rises upon evil men as well as good, and it rains upon the honest and dishonest alike. It's no wonder we hear ourselves saying, "It isn't fair." Sometimes it's hard to make sense out of the world.

I don't want to imply for a second that when tragedy strikes we're supposed to say, "Well, that's the way the cookie crumbles," and then go merrily on with our lives. None of us can do that. At the other extreme, we can't wish pain out of existence, either. What we can do is learn to handle it more effectively. As my friend Tim Hansel says in his wonderful book *You Gotta Keep Dancin'*, "Pain is inevitable, but misery is optional." We can avoid that misery by developing constructive ways of facing up to the pain life deals us. We can resolve that we won't let it destroy us, that we will accept it as a reality of life and even grow from it.

Benjamin Franklin wrote, "Those things that hurt, instruct." Maybe that's why it's often said that some of life's most painful lessons are also the most valuable. The most important thing we can do when we're hurting, whether it's physical or emotional hurt, is to find some meaning in it. Pain does teach us something, but we have to be willing to learn from it. When we do, we emerge as both wiser and stronger. Our real success in life will be largely determined by how well we deal with adversity: whether we run from it or face up to it, whether we shrink or grow from it, whether we surrender to it or triumph over it.

We live in an imperfect world with other imperfect people. No one can promise us lives free from pain or disappointment. Nor can anyone promise us safety or total control. But we're not alone. Every living person shares the same predicament. Every living person encounters unfairness and suffers the hurt and loss which come with it. It's not a question of *whether* they experience these things, but *how* they experience them. The people who succeed in life don't escape unfairness. They just learn to accept it and manage it more constructively.

Maybe that's why so many people have Reinhold Niebuhr's famous Serenity Prayer prominently displayed in their homes and offices:

God grant me . . .

> the serenity to accept the things I cannot change,
> the courage to change the things I can,
> and the wisdom to know the difference.

EVERYDAY COURAGE

What we become depends not on conditions but on decisions. Some people are conditioned and determined by outward circumstances. They're on top when things are going good. They crumble when things go bad. They seem to let the stars, the fates, the gods, the winds, or other things beyond their control determine their lives. What they don't seem to understand is that when we're faced with miserable conditions, we're also faced with a decision: whether to give in to them or stand up to them.

Standing up to some of the harsh realities of life requires courage. Winston Churchill viewed courage as a starting place. He said, "Courage is the first of human qualities because it is the quality which guarantees all the others." He wasn't referring just to courage on a grand scale—that associated with famous people and major events—but everyday courage. No one is born with it, nor does it require any exceptional characteristics. More than anything else, courage is a decision. It's a decision to dig down and search our character, to find a source of strength when life frustrates us. It's the decision we have to make if we want to become fully human.

Shortly before he died, the great theologian and author of *The Courage to Be,* Paul Tillich, was asked to discuss the central theme of his book and to explain the meaning of everyday courage. Tillich said that real courage is saying yes to life in spite of all the hardship and pain which are part of human existence. He said it takes courage on a daily basis to find something ultimately positive and meaningful about both life and ourselves. When we can do that, he said, we not only accept life more fully but begin to live it more fully. "Loving life is perhaps the highest form of the courage to be."

Life is hard . . . and it's not always fair. But that doesn't mean it can't be good, rewarding, and enjoyable. There are still a lot of reasons to say yes to it.

If I were asked to give what I consider the single most useful bit of advice for all humanity it would be this: Expect trouble as an inevitable part of life and when it comes, hold your head high, look it squarely in the eye, and say, "I will be bigger than you. You cannot defeat me."

ANN LANDERS

CHAPTER 3

Life Is Also Fun . . . and Incredibly Funny

Of all the gifts bestowed by nature on human beings, hearty laughter must be close to the top.

NORMAN COUSINS

DISCOVERING THE BALANCE OF LIFE

Now that we've dealt with two of the heavier realities of life, let's look at its lighter and brighter side. We need to appreciate the things which help us stay balanced, which keep us from being crushed under the weight of seriousness, and which we can use to maintain our sanity. I'm talking about another one of the great truths: *Human beings need to have fun.* We need to play, and most importantly, we need to laugh. Life may be hard and at times unfair, but that doesn't mean it has to be intolerable. And it certainly doesn't mean that we can't enjoy it. Humor is what helps the most.

One morning while sitting at my desk laboring over this book and suffering from what appeared to be a terminal case of writer's block, I began to wonder if I had some masochistic tendencies. Writing is one of the most difficult and frustrating things I've ever done, yet I continue to do it. Why was I inflicting this pain on myself? I could be doing other things that were a lot more enjoyable. Like vacuuming or cleaning out the garage. Just then the phone rang. A young woman at the other end asked me, "Is Jeannette there?" I said, "No, Jeannette doesn't live here anymore." "Since when?" she asked. I said, "Didn't you know? Jeannette moved to Bolivia. She went down there to study the mating rituals of the Inca Indians." She then said incredulously, "You've got to be kidding!" I said, "Yeah, I am. I think you dialed the wrong number." The conversation ended when she said, "Man, you're weird!" and hung up.

While she acted somewhat perturbed with me, I have the feeling that she got a chuckle out of our conversation. I certainly did. And I'll bet when she finally did get ahold of Jeannette and told her about the weirdo she talked to, they both had a good laugh. I did, just thinking about their conversation.

In fact, I was wondering if she'd call back to tell me that the Incas lived in Peru, not Bolivia. But I don't think she cared. She and Jeannette probably had more important things to talk about.

The point of all this is that when we get bogged down with some of the ordeals of life, we need a diversion. One of the best is humor. It took me a long time to understand that it's one of the most important ingredients of a healthy and balanced life. I spent years seriously studying the psychology of personal development and fulfillment, only to learn to not take myself so seriously.

During the 1970s, a social phenomenon known as the "personal-growth movement" swept across this country. Led by gurus known as humanistic psychologists, millions of people began the quest for realizing their full potential. The goal in all this was to become "self-actualizing." No one seemed to know exactly what that meant, but it sounded good. It was the key phrase in a decade of psychobabble. Human-potential psychology became the rage, and people went to great extremes (and expense) in order to find their "space," find their "center," and find "themselves." Options included encounter groups and sensitivity training (where people yelled and told each other what they didn't like about them); learning the Maharishi Yogi's style of transcendental meditation (as long as you brought a white hanky, some flowers, and a sizable amount of money); rolfing (I don't think that means throwing up), est (where the leader called people assholes and wouldn't let them go to the bathroom), transactional analysis (in which you learned which "ego state" you were operating from), marijuana smoking, hot-tub soaking, nude massage, and a whole bunch of others. Looking back, it all seems pretty silly. People actually became "growth junkies." Since I was one of them, I can afford to have a good laugh about it. The only unfortunate thing is that I never did learn how to rolf.

I had bought into the movement because, like countless others, I felt something was missing. I was looking for the fulfilled life but never found it in the personal-growth movement. It had become expensive, exhausting, and serious. Too serious. And it actually did more harm than good, because it began to weigh me down. Then a funny and unexpected thing happened. During this time, yet totally unrelated to my relentless search for personal nirvana, I saw two movies which had a more positive and lasting effect on me than all these "growth experiences" put together. Just think, for the price of two movie tickets and about four hours of my time, I could have saved myself a lot of trouble.

The first movie was *Zorba the Greek*. It's the story about a relationship between two men, Zorba and Boss. Boss has looks, intelligence, health, money, and education. He's also a good person who's all locked up inside; he doesn't seem to enjoy life. He reads and he thinks, but he doesn't have fun. He's looking for the missing piece. I found myself identifying with Boss. Then Zorba tells him, "You've got everything, Boss, except one thing: madness. A man needs a little madness or he never does cut the rope and be free." At the end, Zorba teaches Boss to dance, to laugh, and to let go.

The other movie was *A Thousand Clowns*. It's also the story about a relationship, this one between Murray and his eleven-year-old nephew, Nick, whom he is raising alone. Murray's main concern for Nick is that he not grow up to be a Norman Nothing, one of "those nice dead people" who become so serious that they forget how to enjoy life. He wants Nick to be able to see "all the wild possibilities," and to "give the world a little goosing" when he gets the chance. Most important, he wants Nick to look around and to be able to laugh at what he sees.

Most of us need a Zorba or a Murray to remind us to not get bogged down, to not take life and ourselves too seriously. I don't want to imply that either Zorba or Murray are mindless clowns. On the contrary, they're quite deep. They know that life is hard and that it's not always fair, but they also know that the only way to survive it is to get plenty of laughs along the way. And we get those laughs when we *look* for them. Programs like *Candid Camera* and *America's Funniest Home Videos* are funny simply because they hold up a mirror to us. They show us pictures of real life. Life *is* funny. There's comedy all around us. We just have to look for it. As Murray says, there's a need to see ". . . all the cartoons that people make by being alive."

SOME EXAMPLES OF EVERYDAY MADNESS

I had a lot of fun preparing to write this chapter. I read everything I could find on the psychology and benefits of humor and play, and then started reminiscing about things that some of my crazy friends do that make them so endearing. I was having so much fun thinking and laughing about them, I had a hard time getting started with the actual writing. Here are a few examples of intelligent people who have learned the important survival skill of practicing a little madness now and then.

Tim Hansel, mentioned in Chapter 1, is a Stanford graduate and the author of six books. He's philosophical, spiritual, adventurous, and deep. He's also a bit off the wall. When he gets to feeling down, he resorts to his perennial spirit lifter: He yells out the Superman call. You know, the one that goes, "Look, it's a bird! No, it's a plane! No, it's Superman! Up, up, and away!" Now, that may not sound funny to you. But I need to add one more bit of information: Tim yells it backward! This is the way it comes out: "Kool, s'ti a dirb! On, s'ti a enalp! On, s'ti namrepus! Pu, pu, dna yawa!" Try doing that without laughing. Stupid? Yes, very stupid. But also very funny. I heard him speak to a group of businessmen a few years ago. He asked them how much fun they were having in their lives. He also asked them how much fun they were for other people to be with. Then he asked them if they could do the Superman call backward. They looked at him puzzled, so he said it once forward, and then yelled it backward. These heavy hitters of the business world laughed so hard it took him about five minutes to resume his speech.

I have another friend, Russ Sands, who's in his early sixties and is an executive in a major insurance firm in San Francisco. He's educated, drives a big BMW sedan, wears custom-tailored suits, travels around the world representing his company, is a devoted family man, and gives generously of both his time and money to charitable organizations. In other words, he's very sophisticated. He's also one of the funniest and craziest people I've ever known. He finds humor in everything and is a master at making others laugh. He calls things that are funny "a howl," and virtually everything is. He wears red high-top canvas basketball shoes and other items of off-beat clothing. One of his favorite toys used to be a Volkswagen "Thing"—an army-style vehicle that looks like a cross between a Jeep and a Land Cruiser. Now his favorite toy is a Harley-Davidson motorcycle.

He entertains himself and his friends by coming up with wacky expressions. I was at a meeting with him a few years ago when a woman said something which surprised him. He looked at her and said emphatically, "Get a neck!" Where that came from, I'll never know. And several years later, I still haven't figured out what he meant. But he cracked the meeting up, including the woman he was speaking to. Thinking about it still makes me laugh. His most recent expression is, "Time to sack 'em up." It doesn't make sense, either, but it's funny because of the way he says it. Here's a man who works extremely hard and is under great pressure, but he knows how to have a good time. It doesn't really make any difference whether his antics make sense or not. In fact, they're funny because they usually *don't* make sense. That's what humor is: the unexpected, the out-of-character, the absurd.

EDISON AND EINSTEIN

Thomas Edison and Albert Einstein aren't exactly the first two names that come to mind when we think about humor and play. But the fact is that both of them attributed their success in the serious part of life to knowing the importance of the less-serious parts. Both discovered early that to work too hard or to think too intently for an extended period does more harm than good. That's why people need breaks on the job and why students are advised to take study breaks. The mind gets overly stressed when it's subjected to seriousness for too long. Humor and play break the tension.

The stories about Edison's capacity to work long hours and endure thousands of frustrations are almost legendary. What's not as well known are his methods for sustaining himself while working on his famous scientific breakthroughs. Edison kept a cot in his laboratory. He took frequent pauses on it because he knew that only when the mind is in a restful state does it work most creatively. Edison also discovered that humor put his mind at ease. In addition to maintaining hundreds of notebooks full of scientific equations, he filled several others with nothing but jokes. He found that comic relief was valuable for both him and his staff. He used it as a tension breaker and as a morale builder. He said later that people who laugh together can work longer and harder together, and with more effectiveness.

What do we think of when we hear the name Albert Einstein? Genius? Brilliance? Physics? The theory of relativity? Probably all of those. But according to Einstein himself, some of the keys to life were simplicity, fantasy, and play. He said, "Everything should be made as simple as possible." He told a group of Princeton students that he would have no interest in the laws of physics if they couldn't be made simple. One of the ways Einstein kept things simple was through play. Those who have researched his life were surprised to learn what a playful person he was. He literally "fooled around" with ideas and numbers because he knew that his discoveries would eventually come through play. Einstein has a great lesson for us: play is one of the most effective ways of simplifying life. It's what we did so often as children and too often forget to do later in life.

LAUGHTER AS A HEALER

Thousands of years ago a wise man by the name of Solomon wrote his famous Proverbs. Among them, he said, "A cheerful heart is good medicine, but a crushed spirit dries up the bones" (17:22). In modern times, one of the most popular magazines ever published, *Reader's Digest,* contains a section each month entitled "Laughter, the Best Medicine." Is there any scientific evidence to support these claims that laughter has the power of healing in it? Yes.

Only in recent years has the medical profession discovered the almost miraculous healing power of laughter. And the discovery wasn't made by a physician or a medical researcher. It was made by a patient, one who refused to accept a medical prognosis that he had only a few months to live. The patient was Norman Cousins, a well-known writer for *Saturday Review.* Cousins was diagnosed in 1964 as having a serious disease involving the connective tissues. He was also told by a specialist that his chances for survival were one in five hundred and that he had little time to live. But Cousins' will to live was strong, so he decided to assume most of the responsibility for his own healing. He designed a program which required daily use of all the positive emotions. Among them were faith, love, and hope. Cousins said these were easy compared to the other one he knew that had to be part of his healing: laughter. How do you laugh when you've been told you have an irreversible disease and don't have long to live?

But laugh he did. Cousins developed a systematic program for getting daily doses of hearty laughter. He started by watching reruns of the old *Candid Camera* programs. He then went on to Marx Brothers movies and anything else he could get his hands on that would make him laugh. Later, when he wrote of his healing experiences in *Anatomy of an Illness,* Cousins said, "It worked. I made the joyous discovery that ten minutes of genuine belly laughter had an anesthetic effect and would give me at least two hours of pain-free sleep." Medical tests done since then have established that there is a physiological basis for the biblical theory that laughter is good medicine. As Josh Billings, a nineteenth-century humorist, said, "There ain't much fun in medicine, but there's a heck of a lot of medicine in fun."

After his remarkable recovery, Cousins continued to study the effects of positive emotions on the human system. Eventually, he joined the faculty at the UCLA Medical School, a rare appointment for one without an M.D. Cousins also wrote somewhat of a sequel to *Anatomy of an Illness.* It's called *Head First: The Biology of Hope.* In it, Cousins explains more fully the physiological benefits of laughter, especially since more research has been done on it in recent years. He devotes an entire chapter called "The Laughter Connection" to it. Without repeating here the mountains of scientific evidence supporting the theory that laughter is a great healer, let me just summarize the findings of Cousins and the doctors who have worked with him. There is now clear evidence that laughter can be a strong painkiller. In addition, laughter can enhance respiration, produce morphinelike molecules called endorphins, increase the number of disease-fighting immune cells, reduce stress, stimulate the internal organs, and improve the circulation of the blood. Cousins concludes, "Extensive experiments have been conducted, working with a significant number of human beings, showing that laughter contributes to good health. Scientific evidence is accumulating to support the biblical axiom that 'a merry heart doeth good like a medicine.'"

Cousins was one of the pioneers in linking laughter to healing. Since his initial explorations, his research has been duplicated by many both in and out of the medical profession. Best known among them are Dr. Bernie Siegel and Dr. Patch Adams. Both have written extensively about the power of humor and hope in the healing process. If you haven't seen the movie *Patch Adams,* I highly recommend that you rent a copy. It's a little corny in spots, but otherwise heartwarming, funny, and based on scientific evidence.

LAUGHTER AS A WAY OF BEING PRACTICAL

If laughter and the other positive emotions can do all these things for us when we're sick, think what they can do when we're healthy. If it's true that an ounce of prevention is worth more than a pound of cure, then a joyful heart and laughter should be part of our daily routine. If a downcast spirit really does dry up the bones, then we need to keep them greased with some solid belly laughs. Probably the most important discovery about the benefits of laughter is that it can strengthen our immune systems. It has a way of refreshing and revitalizing us. In addition, laughter has been known to soothe jangled nerves, reduce tension, calm tempers, stimulate creativity, and simply make life a lot more fun. Laughter is the tonic of life. It has restorative and invigorating powers. It enlivens and energizes us. It's also an effective lubricant—it can smooth out some of the rough spots of daily existence. Finally, laughter works wonders in relationships. Someone once said that laughter is the shortest distance between two people. It has a way of uniting them. "Laugh, and the world laughs with you."

In one of the classic scenes in *A Thousand Clowns,* Murray asks his brother Arnold why he doesn't do some of the crazy things he did when he was younger, like the time he showed up for work in a fancy suit, a hat, carrying a briefcase . . . and on roller skates. Arnold says, "I don't do practical jokes anymore, if that's what you mean. . . ." Murray jumps up, grabs both of Arnold's arms, and shouts, "PRACTICAL, that's right; a way to stay ALIVE! If most things aren't funny, Arn, then they're only exactly what they are; then it's one long dental appointment interrupted occasionally by something exciting, like waiting or falling asleep."

Actually, laughter is more than practical. It's essential. It's one of the chief ingredients of mental health. We have a genuine need to take a break from life's harsh realities—to act like a nut, to roar with laughter, to delight in the absurd, to chuckle at cartoons, to tell and hear jokes, to see funny movies, and to do wacky things. There's wisdom in the ancient proverb that tells us, "A little nonsense now and then is relished by the wisest of men."

LAUGHTER AS A PRIORITY

I don't want to imply that you have to go through life acting like Daffy Duck or Bozo the Clown in order to be happy. You don't have to wear red high-top basketball shoes or do the Superman call backward, either. We have different personalities and different styles, so we can't all do those kinds of things. But whatever our makeup, we still need an emotional diet which includes play and laughter.

I learned a number of years ago that I was taking life too seriously. In fact, if being serious had been an Olympic sport, my picture would have been on a box of Wheaties. A good friend of mine told me one day that I seemed to be carrying the weight of the world around on my shoulders. He asked me how much fun I was having and how much I laughed. It was at about this time that I saw those two movies mentioned earlier. Zorba taught me about the need to have a little madness now and then, and Murray showed me the importance of seeing the comedy that's all around us. Now this doesn't mean that I turned into some kind of "wild and crazy guy," but laughter did become a high priority in my life. It now ranks right up there with food, sleep, and air. I can't imagine a day without it.

A good place to start is right at home. It's important to be able to laugh at ourselves. Just think for a moment of some of the incredibly stupid, klutzy, harebrained things you've done in your life. Guess what. You're going to do a lot more of them. Don't miss out on the comic character you have within. People who know how to laugh at themselves will never cease to be entertained.

The real key is in looking. There's an old axiom that says we usually find what we're looking for. And there's plenty of comedy and laughter to be found out there. I can't imagine a healthier pursuit.

Laugh and be well.

MATTHEW GREEN

CHAPTER 4

We Live by Choice, Not by Chance

God asks no man whether he will accept life. That is not the choice. You must take it. The only choice is how.

HENRY WARD BEECHER

OUR GREATEST FREEDOM, OUR GREATEST SOURCE OF STRENGTH

Do you realize how many people go through life thinking that the only choices they have are the ones listed in *TV Guide* and on the menu board at McDonald's? Did you know that most people think their place in life has been determined mainly by circumstances, luck, or the way the planets are lined up? The purpose of this chapter is to help you see something they don't. Because too many people never recognize our greatest freedom, which also happens to be our greatest source of strength. And because it's not recognized, it's not used. What is this great freedom, this great source of strength? It's our ability to choose.

It wasn't until I was a junior in college that I began to fully appreciate this as one of the keys to life. Something happened in one of my classes that made me view life differently. I attended the University of San Francisco, a Jesuit school, and was required to take philosophy every semester. The Jesuits, a scholarly order of Catholic priests, were very big on philosophy. They told us that before we went out into the world, they wanted to teach us to think. And they meant it. We were challenged daily to think about God, life, the world, and our place in it. We were required to write papers about the meaning of life and the reason for our existence. We also debated about right and wrong and about good and evil. It was heavy stuff, but it was great training. We learned to better understand life, to accept it as it is, and to deal with it more effectively. And we did, in fact, learn how to think.

On that particular day in class, we were debating the existence of God. It had gone on for quite some time, when one of my classmates challenged the teacher with a question I'd heard many times. He asked, "If God is so good and so powerful, how come he allows all this suffering? Why didn't he just make us so we can be healthy and happy all the time?" The teacher seemed to have been waiting for that one, and I've never forgotten his answer. "If God had created us that way," he said, "we'd be nothing more than puppets. He'd be pulling the strings, and we'd have absolutely no power of our own. It's true, we wouldn't have to experience pain and hardship. But without them, we'd also never know the real triumphs and joys of life. There'd be no reason to find a meaning or a purpose for ourselves. We'd be nothing more than mindless, programmed robots. God did a lot better than that. He created us instead with a free will. He gave us life, and then he gave us the freedom to decide for ourselves what we'll do with it. He gave us the power to choose our own way."

The freedom to decide, the power to choose—what a great lesson in life that was! Yet, how unfortunate it is that so many people never recognize this great freedom or exercise this great power. I've been guilty of it a few times myself, despite that valuable lesson in college. Sadly, we don't always apply what we've been taught. I remember not too many years ago when my life seemed completely out of whack. I was blaming circumstances, rotten luck, and other people. Then I came across the Henry Ward Beecher quote that appears at the beginning of this chapter, and I was reminded that I'd been born with a free will. It wasn't bad circumstances, bad luck, or bad people that were causing my unhappiness. It was bad choices. I had no control over events, but I was still free to choose how to respond to them. When I accepted responsibility for making better choices, life got better.

DISCOVERING OUR CHOICES

Did you know that there are only a few differences between humans and animals? Whether you watch the family dog, an elephant in the zoo, or a mountain goat in the Andes, you'll see that they do essentially the same thing. They eat, sleep, seek shelter, and breed. Those are all instincts. That's what they live by. Their sole purpose is to survive. They react to chance happenings and are conditioned by their environment. That's why it's so easy to train them.

How are we any different? We have the same body parts and functions. And we have the same basic needs, along with the instinct for survival. Like the animals, we react to what happens around us, and we allow ourselves to become conditioned by our environment. And whether we like to admit it or not, we're also easy to train. The only difference is that for us, it doesn't *have* to be that way. We have more than instincts. We have the ability to choose. That's what separates human beings from the animal world. And if we don't exercise that ability, then we're no better off. All we're doing is surviving. Instead of living, we're simply existing.

The starting point for a better life is discovering that we have choices. Sadly, many people never do. They live in a country that offers more freedom of choice than any in the world, yet they live like prisoners, trapped by circumstances. I'm always amazed at some of the excuses people come up with for not taking advantage of life's opportunities to make new choices: not enough money, no time, wrong conditions, poor luck, lousy weather, too tired, bad mood, and the list goes on. But the truth is that they just don't see their choices. It's like being locked up somewhere and having a key in your pocket that'll set you free, but never using it simply because you don't know it's there. You have more choices than you ever dreamed possible. The key is knowing that they're there—every day of your life. We live by choice, not by chance. It isn't what happens that's most important. It's how we deal with what happens. It's what we choose to think and what we choose to do that are most important.

LIFE IS A SERIES OF CHOICES

One way of looking at life is that it's a daily series of choices. In fact, that's the healthiest and most venturesome way I can think of for starting each day. From the time we wake up in the morning until we go to bed at night, we're making choices. If we're not, then someone or something else is making them for us.

I wrote earlier that we all have the potential to do more with our lives. Every human being is capable of making great strides in self-development and major increases in achievement. The starting point for all this is being aware of our choices and then making the right ones. Until those choices are made, nothing is going to happen. Look around you. What *is* happening in the lives of a large percentage of the people in this country? Nothing much. And whether they realize it or not, it's the result of choices: the choice to take what comes, the choice to let things happen, the choice to settle for less, the choice to let others do their thinking, the choice to merely exist from one day to the next.

One of the biggest mistakes people make is thinking that life is one big "have-to." They have to go to work, they have to go to school, they have to go to the store, they have to get their hair cut, they have to get organized, and they have to do a zillion other things. The truth of the matter is that we don't *have* to do anything. Some things might be important, and maybe they should get done, but no one *has* to do them.

It always amazes me how strongly people will argue when told they do everything by choice. They're so stuck on the "have-to" philosophy of life, it's hard for them to let go. I was teaching this concept recently to some high-school seniors in an elective psychology class. The example I used was "You chose to come to class this morning." I would have bet a month's salary that I could predict the first response. And, sure enough, it came. One of my favorite kids in the class said, "No way, man. I *had* to come to class." "No, you didn't," I said. "You *chose* to come." He then proceeded to reel off all the horrible things that would happen to him if he didn't attend class: the school would call his parents, he'd get yelled at at home, he might get grounded, he'd get caught by the vice-principal, his grade would go down, etc. When he was through, I said, "Right! You made a choice. You chose to come to class instead of choosing the consequences of not coming. But you were still free to make that choice. Some of your classmates aren't here. For a variety of reasons, they chose not to come this morning. Maybe someone chose to get some extra sleep or take the whole day off. Maybe someone else chose to go to the doughnut shop. But you chose to be here."

Then he helped me make the most important point of all by

saying, "But that's just another way of looking at it." "Thank you!" I said elatedly. "That's exactly what I want you to learn— to look at every day of your life that way, to see choices instead of have-to's." At any given moment, we're free to choose what to think and what to do. God gave us a free will. No one can take it away from us. We can alter the course of our lives any time we want, because whatever we do, we do by choice. We can say we have to do things or that we're forced to, but the truth is that we do what we choose to do. It's a simple yet great discovery. Because once we realize that we do things by choice, we begin to accept greater responsibility for our own lives and to take more effective control over them. We're the results of our choices.

In both my high-school and university classes I frequently got questions that started with the words, "Do we have to . . . ?" Do we have to know this? Do we have to do that assignment? Do we have to write in complete sentences? Do we have to read that? Do we have to turn it in tomorrow? My answer was always the same: "No. You *get* to." The first time this happened in a new semester, I got some puzzled looks, and occasionally some friendly sarcasm. Then I added the capper: "You don't *have* to do anything in life, but you *get* to do a lot of things. And one of the greatest things you'll ever get to do is become educated." Actually, we ended up having a lot of fun with that one, because for the rest of the semester my students began their questions with the words, "Do we get to . . . ?" I loved it! Because it's really a much healthier way of looking at life. It reminds us that we have choices. We don't *have* to live. We *get* to live.

THE MOST IMPORTANT CHOICES
WE GET TO MAKE

It wasn't our choice to be born into the world. And it's not our choice that someday we're going to die. However, the period in between, the one we call life, presents us with countless choices. There are some obvious ones due to the nature of our society. We can choose our friends, careers, lifestyles, political affiliations, faith, where to live, what kind of car to drive, and what kind of music to listen to. But there are some other choices which, while less obvious, are far more important. We're either unaware of them or just don't give them much thought. Yet, they're the choices that determine the quality of our lives. Based on what life has taught me, these are what I consider to be our most important choices:

- **We're free to choose our character—the type of persons we become.** We can allow ourselves to be molded by others and our environment, or we can commit ourselves to self-development. We can become less than we're capable of, or we can become all that we're capable of.

- **We're free to choose our values.** We can let the media tell us what's important, or we can decide for ourselves. We can base our standards on what others are doing, or we can base them on what we know is right and good.

42

- **We're free to choose how to treat other people.** We can put them down, or we can lift them up. We can be self-centered and inconsiderate, or we can be respectful, kind, and helpful.

- **We're free to choose how to handle adversity.** We can allow ourselves to be crushed, to give up, and to feel sorry for ourselves. Or we can choose to look for a source of strength within us, to persevere, and to make the most out of what life deals us.

- **We're free to choose how much we'll learn.** We can look upon learning as an unpleasant duty or as a great opportunity for bettering ourselves. We can be close-minded or open-minded; we can be stagnant, or we can grow.

- **We're free to choose what we'll accomplish in life.** We can allow our circumstances or other people to determine what we make of ourselves, or we can choose our own direction and goals. We can be undisciplined and lazy, or we can be self-disciplined and hardworking.

- **We're free to choose our own belief system.** We can ignore our spiritual nature, or we can accept it as an important dimension of life. We can worship pleasure and the world's material things, or we can look for something that's ultimately more important.

- **We're free to choose our own purpose.** We can wander aimlessly, or we can search for a meaning in life, and then live according to it. We can live to please only ourselves, or we can find a cause that's greater, one that helps us understand and appreciate life more fully.

- **We're free to choose our attitude regardless of circumstances.** This is the most important choice we'll ever make because it affects everything we do in life. It's explained more fully in the next chapter.

We're Always Choosing

Much of our potential goes to waste simply because it's never used, just like the battery that corrodes or the muscle that atrophies after lying dormant for too long. Most of the time, we fail to exercise our choices because we're not aware of having them. Yet, those choices are available to us every day of our lives. We can make changes in minor aspects of our life, or we can change our entire lifestyle just by making different choices. We can teach ourselves to deal more effectively with both circumstances and with people. In fact, we can change almost anything we do if we're aware of our choices and if our desire is strong enough.

The most important thing to understand about all of this is that at any given moment, we're making choices. Equally important is the need to understand that we're the results of our choices. We can't choose what happens in our lives, but we can choose how to respond. We have the ability to survive hardship and to overcome handicaps. We have the capacity to rise above negative circumstances because we have a free will, the freedom and power to choose. Human beings weren't designed to live by chance. We were designed to live by choice.

The greatest power that a person possesses is the power to choose.

J. MARTIN KOHE

CHAPTER 5

Attitude Is a Choice— the Most Important One You'll Ever Make

Everything can be taken from a man but one thing: the last of the human freedoms—to choose one's attitude in any given set of circumstances, to choose one's own way.

VIKTOR FRANKL

How Can You Have a Good Attitude When Your World Is Caving In?

When I was only twenty-nine, my life was shattered. Something I thought only happened to other people happened to me. My marriage failed. While divorce is a common occurrence in our society, the frequency of it doesn't lessen the hurt and suffering. I've seen lives destroyed by it, and I feared that mine would be one of them. And while the initial pain was devastating, the worst was yet to come. I was told that a man couldn't raise three children and that mine were being taken to live four hundred miles away. I had no voice in the matter. I was in such anguish that I felt both God and our justice system had failed me. Was this really happening? What did I do to deserve it?

As I slowly and painfully began to put the pieces of a broken life back together, a friend gave me something that he thought would help. It was a book called *Man's Search for Meaning* by Viktor Frankl. I have treasured, reread, and given that book to many people since then, because it helped me immeasurably. Reading it didn't restore my marriage or put my family back together, but it helped me think differently about my circumstances. That was one of the most valuable things I've ever learned—that how one thinks about events is far more important than the events themselves.

In the midst of my agony, I learned that Dr. Frankl's circumstances had been much worse. Yet, by using his free will and the powers of his mind, he was able to overcome them. Frankl was one of the millions of Jews placed in Nazi concentration camps during World War II. The Hitler regime took virtually everything away from him: his wife, children, home, medical practice, and all of his worldly possessions. He was thrown into a prison camp where he experienced every form of human degradation possible. Frankl watched several of his friends be killed in that concentration camp. He also saw many men commit suicide, while others simply lost the will to live, gave up, and died. Frankl wrote later that amidst all the brutality and suffering, what bothered him the most was to see his fellow prisoners decide that there was nothing left to live for, and then give up on life.

He was determined to find something he still had that the Nazis couldn't take, something important enough to sustain his will to live. He decided there was one thing that no one could take away—his ability to choose his own attitude—no matter how bad his conditions became. Viktor Frankl not only survived the atrocities of this camp and the war, but he also went on to become one of the most respected psychiatrists the world has ever known. He's helped thousands of people who were ready to give up on life gain a renewed will to live by showing them that they still have choices, and that within those choices they can find new meaning in their lives.

He calls the ability to choose our own attitude in any given set of circumstances ". . . the last of the human freedoms." He says even in the prison camp there were always choices to make. "Every day, every hour, offered the opportunity to make a decision, a decision which determined whether you would or would not submit to those powers which threatened to rob you of your very self, your inner freedom." Frankl says we can become the victim of circumstances or we can be victorious over them. We can renounce our freedom and dignity and let our circumstances mold us, or we can choose our own attitude and rise above them. The key, he says, is knowing that what we become is the effect of an inner decision.

As a result of reading that book and help from friends,

I changed my attitude about my circumstances. It went from one of defeat and gloom to one of optimism and hope. I was determined to make the most out of my life in spite of the loss. The only other choice I had was to let it destroy me.

I was also determined to live with my sons again, and never a day went by that I didn't believe that would happen. Two years after the divorce, all three of them returned to me. I then struck a blow for the equal-rights movement by proving that a man *could* raise three children. It wasn't the ideal family situation that I'd always envisioned, but we made the most of our circumstances. Instead of feeling sorry for ourselves, we found reasons to be thankful. It was a struggle (life is hard), but we had a great time, mostly because we had great attitudes!

WHY ATTITUDE IS SO IMPORTANT

Near the end of the previous chapter, I wrote that attitude is the most important choice we'll ever make because it affects everything we do in life. Research conducted at Harvard and several other top universities bears this out. I read about several studies while taking courses in the psychology of "peak performance" at Stanford in the late 1990s. The major findings were that attitude is far more important than intelligence, education, special talent, or luck. The people who did this study concluded that up to eighty-five percent of our success in life is due to attitude, while the other fifteen percent is due to ability. While it's difficult to assign specific percentages to these kinds of traits, anyone who has studied human behavior would agree that the starting point for all success is forming a good attitude. William James, one of the most practical and respected of all American psychologists, said, "The greatest discovery of my generation is that human beings can alter their lives by altering their attitudes." Even country singing star Hank Williams, Jr., tells us that we'll be fine as long as we get regular "attitude adjustments." It's important, then, to understand just what attitude is.

Attitude is a mental outlook, a frame of mind. It's how we think. It's what goes on inside a person—thoughts and feelings—about self, others, circumstances, and life in general. Attitude is similar to a mood or a disposition. It's also an expectancy. People who have generally positive attitudes expect the best; people with negative attitudes expect the worst. In both cases, those expectations are usually fulfilled.

The late broadcaster and author Earl Nightingale described attitudes as "reflections of people." What goes on inside invariably shows on the outside; it's reflected in what we say and do. Our attitudes also operate somewhat like magnets. We're pulled in the direction of our thoughts, whether they're positive or negative. We usually get what we expect because the thoughts we choose set the wheels in motion and then move us in a particular direction. To some extent, it's the old rule of cause and effect: a good attitude gets good results; a bad attitude gets bad results. People who succeed regularly expect to succeed. They develop the habit of expecting good things to happen, and they know that the primary vehicle for taking them where they want to go is the mind.

The key point I made in Chapter 2 was that the world won't

devote itself to making us happy. It doesn't function to please us, nor will it adapt to our needs and wants. We have to form an attitude that reminds us that it's our responsibility to adapt to the world in such a way that those needs and wants can still be satisfied. We can do that by developing a positive and real-istically expectant outlook on life. We can't adjust situations to fit our lives perfectly, but we can adjust our attitudes to fit all situations. We can learn to do this because all attitudes, whether good or bad, are learned. No one was born with any particular attitude. It was developed over time. Where we are today is the result of the attitudes we've learned (chosen). If we want to change it, we need to start by changing our attitudes and learning new ones.

The most important thing I learned from reading Frankl's book was that we can direct our thoughts to work for us or to work against us. They can be our best friends or our worst enemies. They can provide us with a positive outlook, attract people to us, and greatly improve our chances for success. On the other hand, they can produce a negative outlook, repel people from us, and doom our chances for success. That's why attitude is the most important choice we'll ever make.

YOUR ATTITUDE IS WHAT YOU SAY WHEN YOU TALK TO YOURSELF

If you're like everyone else, you talk to yourself a lot. I don't know if anyone has ever done a study on it, but I'd guess that we talk to ourselves more than half the time when we're alone.

It might be because we enjoy good conversation, or we just like talking to intelligent people. Whatever the reason, we all engage in self-talk. And what we say to ourselves has more impact than what others say to us. We form thoughts and feelings based on what we tell ourselves, and we eventually act on those thoughts and feelings. Our self-talk is our attitude.

Some years ago, when I was hunting for some interesting perspectives on attitude, an intriguing book title caught my eye. It was *What to Say When You Talk to Your Self.* It's written by Shad Helmstetter, an authority on self-management and a consultant to corporations and organizations throughout the world. The book turned out to be as good as the title, and it contains some great advice for developing a healthy attitude. Helmstetter sees attitude as the key to effectively managing anything—an organization, a career, a home, or an individual life. This is because everything we do is affected by our attitudes. A change in attitude can result in drastic changes in one's life. And it isn't just Hank Williams, Jr., who thinks we need occasional attitude adjustments. Helmstetter claims that even small attitude adjustments can profoundly affect what we do and how we do it. He thinks attitude is so important, he calls it the deciding factor in whether we're to succeed in life or not. "The right attitude gives us that important edge," he says.

Helmstetter is convinced that a good attitude is the principal ingredient of a good life. He makes his point:

> *Our attitudes propel us forward toward our victories or bog us down in defeat. They are the foothold beneath us in*

every step we take. They are what others see most of the personality within us; they describe us and define us, projecting the image we present to the world around us. Our attitudes make us rich or poor, happy or unhappy, fulfilled or incomplete. They are the single most determining factor in every action we will ever make. We and our attitudes are inextricably combined; we are our attitudes and our attitudes are us.

THREE GREAT WAYS TO APPROACH LIFE

Golfers know that the success of their game is determined by how they approach the ball. Pilots know that the most critical part of landing a plane is in making the right approach. Lawyers know that how they approach the jury will be a determining factor in each case. Approaching means getting ready, taking the preliminary steps toward some type of achievement. The right approach to anything sets the stage for creating the results we hope for. In essence, our attitudes are the way we approach life. And the way we approach it will determine our success or failure.

Based on everything I've ever done, read, heard, and seen, I'm convinced that there are three great ways to approach life. They're three of the most important choices we can ever make. They're three of the best attitudes we can ever have. I guarantee that the more you use these three approaches, the more success you'll find in life.

1. Think with an open mind

An open mind is the beginning of self-discovery and growth. We can't learn anything new until we can admit that we don't already know everything.

ERWIN G. HALL

I was a philosophy minor in college, so I took a lot of courses that required me to think at a deeper level than I'd been used to. It all began with a course in logic. The professor said the purpose of logic was to get us to think straight, to examine all sides of an issue, and to be able to arrive at conclusions based on sound reasoning. He said he was going to train us in good thinking habits. Then he said something that I've never forgotten: "But I can't teach you a thing if you don't come to class with an open mind. In fact, you'll never learn anything until you learn to open your mind."

Naturally, there were questions. We were fresh out of high school, had never really been challenged to think, and weren't even sure what an open mind was. The professor, a wise and kind Jesuit, said, "An open mind is an attitude. It means you don't think you already know everything. That's the trouble with too many young people. They learn a little and then think they know everything. Their minds shut down, and nothing new gets in. They become know-it-alls. That's the worst mistake you can make."

He also wanted us to understand that an open mind isn't the same thing as an empty head. He re-emphasized that open-mindedness is an attitude, the key to all learning and personal development. He said the purpose of an education isn't to *fill* our minds but to *open* them. The more knowledge we have, the more we realize how much we don't know. This is what open-mindedness is. It helps us to see all sides, to be more understanding, and to be aware of our own limitations.

It was a great course and a good introduction to philosophy and real thinking. I still remember his final words: "If you didn't learn anything else, I hope you learned this one thing: Think with an open mind."

2. Think for yourself

Don't let the world around you squeeze you into its own mold.

ROMANS 12:2

Believe me, the world works extremely hard at doing just that. And it has thousands of slick devices today that it didn't have when St. Paul wrote that advice to his friends. Without any effort or even realizing that it's happening, we can turn our lives into exercises in mindless conformity: go with the flow, be in, be cool. In other words, let others do our thinking for us. I know how easy it is because I've been there. It's like getting into a big circle and following the follower to nowhere.

If the ability to choose is our greatest freedom and source of strength, then we can't afford to give up the right to choose our thoughts. They're our most valuable resource. The media, the advertising world, and other people try to do our thinking for us every day. They'll take over our minds if we let them. But we have a choice. If we pay attention to what's going on around us, we can screen out the trash and preserve the right to think for ourselves. We can choose our own thoughts and, with them, our own beliefs, values, and priorities. We can do the things that are right instead of the things everyone else is doing.

One of Ralph Waldo Emerson's most famous writings is an essay called "Self-Reliance." It's a powerful statement about the need to think for ourselves. He felt, even in the 1840s, that too many people take the easy way out by choosing ". . . to live after the world's opinion." But when we do that, we give up all right to ourselves. We need to develop and appreciate our own character, not let it be shaped by someone or something else. If we let others do our thinking for us, we'll never experience what Emerson calls the integrity of our own minds. He concludes his essay with "Nothing can bring you peace but yourself. Nothing can bring you peace but the triumph of principles."

3. Think constructively

The thinker knows he is today where his thoughts have taken him and that he is building his future by the quality of the thoughts he thinks.

WILFRED ARLAN PETERSON

Does positive thinking work? Not always, but it's a lot more effective than negative thinking is. Actually, they both work to a degree. They set the wheels in motion for fulfilling our expectations. Positive thinking has a nice ring to it, but to most people it's really just *wishful* thinking. That's why it doesn't always work. Positive thinking has to be accompanied with genuine belief. Believing is a mental and spiritual process which is deeper than the average person's notion of what positive thinking is. People who succeed in life don't *think* they can; they *believe* they can. That belief in themselves doesn't result from isolated incidents of positive thinking. It develops over a period of time, builds on itself, and eventually becomes a way of life.

That's why I prefer the term constructive thinking. While similar to positive thinking, it takes into account the fact that no one can have positive thoughts a hundred percent of the time. That's as unrealistic as it is impossible. Constructive thinkers are aware of negative ideas clamoring for attention but don't allow themselves to be dragged down by them. Instead, they train themselves to choose thoughts which build character and lead to personal achievement.

In recent years, the human mind has been compared to a computer. Both are marvelous instruments, but they only work well when fed the right information. Computer programmers have an acronym called GIGO: "garbage in, garbage out." The mind operates the same way. It has to be fed with useful information in order to function at maximum efficiency. Constructive thinkers know this. They're careful in selecting the information which is fed into their minds. They're also careful in keeping out the garbage. It's an effective way of choosing the right thoughts.

Your ability to choose, especially to choose your own attitude, is the most important resource you have for succeeding in life. The best advice I have is to think with an open mind, think for yourself, and think constructively.

Your living is determined not so much by what life brings to you as by the attitude you bring to life; not so much by what happens to you as by the way your mind looks at what happens.

JOHN HOMER MILLER

CHAPTER 6

Habits Are the Key to All Success

In truth, the only difference between those who have failed and those who have succeeded lies in the difference of their habits.

OG MANDINO

THE POWER OF HABIT

We're creatures of habit. In all the years I've been hearing that old expression, I've never heard anyone dispute it. Probably because there's so much truth to it. In fact, we're even more the result of habit than most people realize. Some psychologists believe that up to ninety-five percent of our behavior is formed through habit. While someone might argue that particular figure, I doubt that anyone would disagree that our habits have a powerful hold on us. Most of them start innocently and unintentionally. At the beginning they form a kind of invisible thread. But through repetition, that thread becomes entwined into a cord and later into a rope. Each time we repeat an act, we add to it and strengthen it. The rope becomes a chain and then a cable. Eventually, we become our habits. As English poet John Dryden said over three hundred years ago, "We first make our habits, and then our habits make us."

The original meaning of *habit* was "garment," or "piece of clothing." And as with garments, we wear our habits daily. Our personalities are actually a composite of our attitudes, habits, and appearance. In other words, our personalities are the characteristics by which we're identified, the parts of us which we reflect to others. As with our clothes, all of our habits are acquired. We're not born with any of them. We learn them, just as we learn our attitudes. They develop over time and are reinforced through repetition.

It's not my purpose to offer a scientific explanation of how and why we form habits. I just want to point out that we all do. Habits are part of being human. No one escapes them. I don't advise people to avoid forming habits. They couldn't anyway. I advise them to think about the kinds of habits they're forming. Whether we like it or not, we become slaves to our habits. They end up working either for us or against us.

I think one of the real problems is that there's never been enough emphasis placed on forming good habits. The only time we ever hear the words *good* and *habit* in the same sentence is when a teacher comments on the need for good study habits. If good habits lead to success in school, then they'll lead to success in other areas of life. But, unfortunately, our bad habits get most of the attention, which only reinforces them. We need to change our focus to the positive side of habits and put more energy into building good ones. Seeing their rewards can help us do that.

WINNING HABITS

I was taught about the importance of good habits both in high school and in college. But I didn't learn them in the classroom; I learned them on the basketball court. I had a genuine passion for the game, and loved putting the ball through the hoop. But an outstanding high-school coach taught me that the game had other aspects: footwork, defense, positioning, rebounding, and passing. He told me when I was a freshman that if I wanted to become good enough to play in college, I had to be a complete player, not just a shooter. He said, "You develop those skills by learning to do them correctly and then by repeating them over and over. The more you repeat them, the easier it'll be to do them right when it counts in the games. They'll come automatically if you form good habits."

That was his way of letting me know that basketball wouldn't always be fun. In practice it would be hard work, drill, conditioning, and pain. It would be repeating the same movements over and over and over. One day when we were doing our most hated drill he said, "I want you guys to do this so often that you'll be doing it in your sleep." And I can remember to this day doing just that. I would wake up feeling tired because I'd been doing defensive footwork drills all night long. The result of all this was that good habits were formed. And just as the coach had said, when game time came around, we automatically did the right things. Those skills didn't come to us naturally. They came as the result of what he'd said would determine our success: forming winning habits.

When I got to college I had the privilege of playing for one of the most successful coaches ever. Phil Woolpert had led USF to back-to-back NCAA championships in the mid-1950s and was one of the most respected men in the profession. Because of him, my education in the value of good habits was raised to a higher level. Those painful drills in high school were only a warm-up for what Phil was going to teach me. There was one drill that he called "hands up." It involved getting our feet in position, bending at the knees, putting one hand high above our head and the other one out to the side. Then we moved quickly forward, backward, to the left, or to the right at his command. We called this drill "time in hell" because it was sheer pain and seemed to last for eternity. But we always played good defense because we were ready; our feet, knees, and hands automatically went into the right position. Like my high-school coach, Phil believed that forming good habits was the key to success.

And it didn't apply just to the basketball court. When I was a sophomore, he taught me something that I've never forgotten. We were working on a play in which I broke to a spot under the basket, received a pass, and quickly went up for an easy shot. The only problem was that the guy defending me blocked it. Phil stopped the action and pointed out that had I not done a few little things wrong, I would have had the two points. When I'd received the pass, I looked down at the floor, bounced the ball once, and then went up for the shot. He pointed out that what I'd done was give the defensive man time to get ready for me. He told me to get into the habit of keeping my hands, my head, and my eyes up; then go immediately for the shot. He said that developing little habits like that could make a big difference in my overall effectiveness. Then he added, "Good habits make the difference, not just in the gym, but in everything we do."

Here was a man I greatly admired, teaching me about a game I loved. And in the process, he gave me one of my most valuable lessons in life. Phil wasn't respected merely because his teams won games. He was respected because of the principles by which he coached and lived. Soon after he made the comment about habits making the difference in everything we do, I realized what it was that I admired about him so much. His high principles were actually his own habits, the successful things he did every day. Phil died a few years ago, and my playing days are long over with, but a good teacher's influence remains forever. He taught me that good habits really *do* make the difference in everything we do. We don't succeed by doing something right one time; we succeed by doing things right on a regular basis. Habits are the key to all success.

CHANGING HABITS

Whenever I teach or speak on this topic, I always point out that, like attitudes, habits can be changed. And neither the age of the person nor the length of the habit can be used as an argument for holding on to it. The only thing that matters is desire. Invariably, someone asks me, "Haven't you heard that you can't teach an old dog new tricks?" I answer yes, I've heard that old expression many times, but a number of dog trainers have proven it wrong. Besides, my message isn't for old dogs, and it isn't about tricks. It's for people, and it's about habits.

More than twenty years ago, I changed a habit that I'd had for more than thirty years. It was swearing. I'm embarrassed to say now that for all that time I never thought there was anything wrong with it. "Everybody does it, and they're just words anyway" was my rationale. But a friend whom I greatly admired confronted me gently one day with it. He asked me if I realized that the words I used revealed something about myself. He asked me if it had ever occurred to me that some of the words were offensive to others. And he asked me if I might not be able to communicate better by choosing more effective ones. I had nothing to say that could justify my swearing. So after thinking about it for a while, I stopped, just like that. Why? First, because I saw the need. My language was offensive to others and harmful to me. Second, because I had a strong enough desire. The more I'd thought about what my friend said, the more I wanted to make a change.

I don't mean to imply that all long-standing habits can be

stopped this easily. Going "cold turkey" works for some people but not for others. Actually, it's the exception rather than the rule, especially when the habits are such things as drinking, smoking, or using drugs. But the starting points still have to be the same: seeing the need and having the desire. If they're not there, all the help in the world will go to waste.

Trying to break a bad habit through sheer willpower rarely works. What has proven to be far more effective is replacing the habit—substituting it with a behavior that's more positive. This technique has been around for hundreds of years, at least as far back as Benjamin Franklin's time. In his famous autobiography, Franklin explains a technique he used for eliminating his worst habits and replacing them with good ones. He made a list of thirteen qualities he wanted to have. He put them in order of importance and wrote each one on a separate page in a small notebook. He concentrated on each quality for a week at a time. If he failed to practice that particular virtue satisfactorily, he would record little black marks next to it. By working steadily at each one, he eventually eliminated the need to make the marks. By this time he had acquired the virtue. By using this technique, Franklin's new habits replaced some of his old ones. He eliminated a set of behaviors that worked against him while acquiring another set that was more beneficial to him. He said it made him realize that he had more faults than he'd originally thought, but the experiment had also given him great satisfaction in seeing their replacements take over. Franklin, through a conscious effort, acquired better habits. In doing so, he became a better person.

HABIT AND CHARACTER

I became interested in the role habit plays in our lives as a result of my early training on the basketball court. Especially since that day more than thirty years ago when Phil Woolpert said, "Good habits make the difference . . . in everything we do." As I began to make some important discoveries about life in my late thirties, I also began to understand that there's a relationship among habits, character, and real success. As George Dana Boardman said, "Sow an act . . . reap a habit; sow a habit . . . reap a character; sow a character . . . reap a destiny."

As my own habits and character improved, so did my quality of life. As a teacher of courses in human behavior, it was natural to want to share these discoveries with my students, both in the high school and at the university. But a teacher can't establish a theory based solely on his own experiences. There has to be evidence to support it, so I scoured libraries and bookstores for writings on habit. To my surprise, not many books have been written about habit, despite its importance. However, the two I discovered both reinforced my belief that our habits reflect our character.

The first one was *Habits of the Heart,* by sociologist Robert Bellah and four associates. They write that ". . . the kind of life we want depends on the kind of people we are—on our character." It isn't what we have or the techniques we use that make us successful. It's who we are. The habits that matter most are the ones that involve our connectedness to other people and the rest of the world. People with high principles and good character have such habits as integrity, concern for others, service, and commitment. They know that the good life is impossible if we look out only for ourselves. It's earned, not by taking from life, but by contributing to it.

The other book is *The 7 Habits of Highly Effective People,* by Stephen R. Covey. Covey's subtitle is *Restoring the Character Ethic.* His point is that too many people are seduced by what he calls outward success. They attain it but still end up feeling empty. They learned methods by which to obtain things but didn't develop the principles and habits that result in feelings of self-worth and fulfillment. When our country was still new, we concentrated on teaching young people the Character Ethic. But we moved away from it as people looked for quicker ways to acquire material wealth. Covey sees a need to return to what made us great as a people and as a country. His premise is: "The Character Ethic taught that there are basic principles of effective living, and that people can only experience true success and enduring happiness as they learn and integrate these principles into their basic character."

Good habits make the difference in everything we do. They're the key to real success.

We are what we repeatedly do. Excellence, then, is not an act, but a habit.

ARISTOTLE

CHAPTER 7

Being Thankful Is a Habit—the Best One You'll Ever Have

Don't complain because you don't have. . . . Enjoy what you've got.

H. STANLEY JUDD

WHAT GETS YOUR ATTENTION?

How many times a day do you complain? If you're anything like my students were, both in the high school and in the university, the number is pretty high. That's not a criticism of my students, just a statement of the way things are. I did some experiments with my classes and my speaking audiences for many years, and they proved that there's a lot of truth in philosopher Arthur

Schopenhauer's claim that "we seldom think of what we have but always of what we lack."

The first one is a simple exercise—simple to explain, but not to do. I asked my students to go the next twenty-four hours without complaining. The first response is usually a complaint about the assignment. After getting that out of the way, we discuss some of the particulars. My first suggestion was that they not stop the experiment if they blew it and complained within the first hour (because most of them did). If they couldn't go twenty-four hours without complaining, I wanted them at least to see how few complaints they could make in one day. So I suggested that they carry a piece of paper with them while they were trying it and write down each time they complained and each time they caught themselves about to complain.

The following day we discussed the results of the assignment. I asked the students to guess how many people were able to keep from complaining since the day before. They all wrote a number down, and I did the same. In a class of thirty, their predictions usually ran between six and twelve. My own prediction was always a zero. And it was always the correct one because I had the advantage of knowing what happened all the previous times. It took twenty-three years before I finally found a student who could do it. By a conservative estimate, I've now challenged more than seventy thousand people of all ages to try this. At last count, I'd found four who didn't complain.

The best part of the experiment, though, was the discussion that followed. I asked two simple questions: What was the purpose of the assignment? What did you learn from trying it? There was virtually always agreement on the answers to both. The answer to the first question usually goes like this: "You wanted to show us how much we complain." Right. The second one is usually: "I learned that I don't really have much to complain about. What I complain about is stupid." Right again. Whether they actually made the complaint or caught themselves about to complain, they got in touch with both how frequent and how puny their complaints were.

But that was only part one of the assignment. Part two began right after the discussion. I gave the students a piece of paper that read "I'm thankful for . . ." across the top. It had three columns below. The first column was labeled "Things." Below it they were asked to list all the material things they were glad they had. The second one said "People." They listed all the people they appreciated. The third one said "Other." Below it they listed anything they were thankful for that didn't fit in the first two columns. The Things and People columns got filled up quickly: the Other column took longer. I got questions like "What do you mean?" and "Can you give us some ideas?" So, I asked for some of their ideas to help us get started. These are some of the "others" that emerged: freedom, opportunity, friendship, love, intelligence, abilities, health, talents, peace, faith, God, security, learning, experiences, beauty, kindness, and the list continues. In about twenty minutes, all three columns were full.

Part three of the assignment began immediately. Within the next twenty-four hours, they were asked to read their lists four times: after lunch, after dinner, before going to sleep, and the next morning before going to school or work. When they arrived the next day, I asked if they felt any different than they did the day before, after trying not to complain. Actually, I already knew the answer. Their body language coming into class was significantly different, not only from the day before but from any previous day. There were more and bigger smiles, eyes were open wider, and bodies were more alive. Magic? No, just appreciation. Thankfulness does wonders for the soul. All we need to do is ask ourselves what's getting our attention. When we focus on what's right instead of what's wrong, life improves considerably.

In writing this, I don't know whether I've captured the real spirit of these exercises. If I was explaining it in person, I'd be jumping up and down, yelling, and waving my arms like Dick Vitale announcing a college basketball game on ESPN! I get that excited about what happens during this forty-eight-hour period. It still amazes me, after more than thirty years of doing it, how effective it was in waking people up to what they have and to why they can be thankful. In fact, this was one of the two best assignments I'd ever given in my teaching career. (The other one is explained in Chapter 10.)

I want to make special mention of how much adults profit from these simple exercises. Originally, I used this technique only at the high-school level. But the truth is, adults complain more than kids do. So I thought I'd give it a try with them. Keep in mind that many of my university students were in their thirties and forties. Their response was even more dramatic than that of my high-school students. It's probably because they've been taking things for granted for a much longer time. They raved so much about the value of that exercise at the end of the course, you'd think I'd discovered the meaning of life. I wouldn't go that far, but I may have helped them discover something that not only adds meaning to life, but also makes it a lot more enjoyable.

Being thankful, if practiced regularly, becomes a habit. It's the best one we can have because it's the healthiest possible way of looking at life. It's not just a habit, but an attitude. Being able to appreciate what we have is one of the keys to fulfillment. Real enjoyment starts with being thankful. Maybe that's why the Bible tells us that we need to begin our prayers by thanking instead of asking.

Isn't it too bad that Thanksgiving comes only once a year? It's the only time we're asked to stop and think about all that we have and to celebrate it with loved ones. But there's really no reason why we can't do that every day of the year. We don't have to declare a holiday and eat a turkey in order to celebrate our blessings. Would your own life be any different if you had one of those three-column lists and read it four times a day? I think it would, and there's an easy way to find out if I'm right. It would take about twenty minutes to fill in the three columns, and a few minutes a day to read it over.

It works. I promise. It's a great starter kit for learning how to become more appreciative. Like other thoughts and actions that are frequently repeated, being thankful can become a way of life. That is, if we choose it as an attitude and make it a habit.

Appreciating What We Have

Benjamin Franklin said we never appreciate the value of water until the well runs dry. That's true with a lot of other things, too. It's easy to take people, things, and freedom for granted, especially if we've never been without them. Sometimes going without can be a great teacher. Eddie Rickenbacker, the famous World War I pilot, once drifted in a life raft for twenty-one days in the Pacific Ocean, hopelessly lost. He survived the ordeal and was asked later if it had taught him anything. He said, "The biggest lesson I learned from that experience was that if you have all the fresh water you want to drink and all the food you want to eat, you ought never to complain about anything." Unfortunately, we snivel and complain about piddling little things that other people would be happy about. This too can become a habit, a way of life. Don't we all know at least a few constant complainers? They're not exactly fun to be around, are they?

There are groups of high-school and college students in my area who go to Mexico every year to help build small houses for the poor. They always return from that experience with some new perspectives on life. They see how hard things are for the Mexican peasants who lack many of the things we consider necessities. But they also see how thankful and joyful these people are for what little they *do* have. These students come home with a good feeling because they helped less fortunate people. But they also come home with a greater appreciation of how much they themselves have.

Unfortunately, we need to experience firsthand how the

rest of the world lives in order to fully understand how truly blessed we are. It's sad that we've become immune to the pictures we see of starving people in other parts of the world as well as at home. It doesn't have an impact until we're face-to-face with it. Some years ago my wife, Cathy, and I were in China. We took a four-hour bus trip from a port near Hong Kong to Canton, a major city in the southern part of the country. I'd seen countless pictures of life in China, but this experience shook me. As I wrote in my journal about what I was seeing and feeling, I had to grope for the right words. Finally, I came up with *squalor* and *hopelessness.* For hundreds of miles all I saw on each side of the road was a misery that was beyond my comprehension. No matter how many times we're told and no matter how many pictures we see, the full impact hits us only when we experience it ourselves. It made me think of my "no complaining" exercise, and I wrote this in my journal: "I wish there were several buses behind us filled with all my students, both the kids and the adults. I wish they could see this. I wouldn't have to say a thing about appreciating what they have. They'd go home with more gratitude than they'd ever felt. I'll bet none of them would have any trouble going a day without complaining."

Some of my colleagues in the teaching profession had spent a year or more working for the Peace Corps or as missionaries in underdeveloped countries. Without exception, they say that those were the most valuable learning experiences of their lives. They learned the joy of giving rather than just taking, and they learned to better appreciate the rich abundance in their own lives. Some countries require all their young people to spend time in military service. I wish we required all our young people to spend at least one year in service to others. What a great way that would be to start adulthood! And what a way to learn to appreciate what we have!

THINK, BUT DON'T FORGET TO THANK

In many of the Cromwellian churches in England, there are two words engraved in the stone walls: *THINK* and *THANK.* I wish we had those two words posted as reminders all around us: in our homes, in our cars, in our schools, and in our places of work. Maybe they would help us think about what we have. That's what the first part of this chapter has been about: *THINK* about what we have, and develop an attitude of thankfulness.

This part is about *THANK.* While I fervently urge you to think often of what you have, I urge you with an equal passion to use the magic words "thank you" every chance you get. I'm not alone in my belief that thanking others seems to be a dying art. Whether it's a general decline in good manners or the attitude of many people that they're entitled to service and things from others, we don't hear that special phrase as much as we used to. Yet, showing our appreciation to others is one of the highest expressions of respect and courtesy. It's also one of the surest ways of building and maintaining solid relationships. William James said, "The deepest principle in human nature is the craving to be appreciated." And it's as easy as it is rewarding to satisfy that need in others.

Of our countless blessings, among the greatest are the special people who enrich our lives every day. All of us know people who have a way of lifting our spirits, teaching us something, bringing out the best in us, and simply making us feel better. Because of them we try harder, function better, and live more fully. Obviously, we appreciate them. But do we tell them?

If you were asked to make a list of the people you appreciate the most, wouldn't it be an easy task to write down their names? And if you were asked why you appreciate them, wouldn't it be just as easy to write the reasons after each name? Now for a more difficult question. Could you write after each name on your list the last time you told that person you appreciate him or her? What would be the result? There might be some awkward feelings at first. We have rather extensive vocabularies for complaining and expressing anger, but we get tongue-tied when it comes to expressing our appreciation. That's because we've practiced the former so many more times. But if you can work past the awkwardness, you're going to make two people feel very good: the person you're thanking and yourself. It's a double-win situation.

It's one thing to appreciate people. It's quite another to thank them. Have you ever noticed that we usually only say good things about people when they're not around? Why do we tell other people? Why not tell the ones we appreciate? Why waste those feelings of thankfulness? When someone dies, everyone else seems to have something good to say. I often wonder how many of those compliments were heard by the person while he or she was still alive? Did we take the time to express our appreciation? Do people have to die to wake us up to how special they are to us? We need to express our thanks more often to those special people in our lives.

We also need to develop the habit of saying thank you to the people outside our circle of friends and family. I cringe when I see the way people who work in gas stations, stores, and hotels get treated by many of their customers. Here they are working for a living and helping us, but they're often treated as if they're non-persons completely devoid of feelings. Yet, how simple it is to say thank you. In a matter of seconds, we can make someone else's day simply by showing our gratitude. People do have a powerful need to be appreciated.

I think we also have the need to *express* our appreciation. My mom, probably the world's most grateful person, taught me that it wasn't real thankfulness if it wasn't expressed. This was one of the earliest and most valuable lessons I received while growing up. She didn't teach me this by telling; she taught me by doing. I don't think an opportunity to express appreciation has ever slipped by her. She tells people in person, phones them, and writes thank-you notes. She even writes *me* thank-you notes! She has a reputation for being a kind and gracious lady. One of the main reasons is that she's mastered the art of saying thank you. She always makes other people feel appreciated.

Being thankful and saying thanks are two habits of people who've discovered what it means to succeed in life. Learning to appreciate is one of the most important steps leading to fulfillment.

FIVE THINGS TO BE THANKFUL FOR

My goal in teaching about thankfulness as an attitude and as a habit was to help people develop a greater awareness and appreciation of what they had. At the same time, I was always curious to learn what they were most thankful for after thinking about all of this and doing the exercises. At the end of the unit, I asked them to list their "Top 5." There was strong agreement among both the high-school kids and the adults whom I taught in college. While other things appeared on some of the lists, these were the consensus choices:

1. Special people
2. Freedom of choice
3. Boundless opportunity
4. Education and learning
5. General abundance and quality of life

Not a bad list! It makes a great starting place for becoming more thankful.

It is not how much we have but how much we enjoy. . . .
CHARLES SPURGEON

CHAPTER 8

Good People Build Their Lives on a Foundation of Respect

Treat other people exactly as you would like to be treated by them. . . .

MATTHEW 7:12

RESPECT FOR LIFE

One of the greatest human beings who ever lived left us one of the greatest phrases ever written. His name was Albert Schweitzer, and the phrase was his philosophy: "reverence for life." Sadly, Schweitzer isn't as well known as he should be. He ranks right up there with Socrates, Buddha, Lincoln, Gandhi, and Mother Teresa. In fact, he was the Mother Teresa of his time (1875–1965). Like her, he was awarded the Nobel Peace Prize for humanitarian service. Schweitzer was also a musician, philosopher, physician, missionary, and theologian.

One of the things Schweitzer struggled with for many years was the formation of a philosophy that captured the essence and meaning of life. In his autobiography, he tells the story of making a slow and difficult 160-mile trip on a small steamer up an African river in 1915: "Late on the third day, at the very moment when, at sunset, we were making our way through a herd of hippopotamuses, there flashed upon my mind, unforeseen and unsought, the phrase, 'Reverence for Life.' " The following day, while still on the boat and alone with his thoughts, he defined this phrase for which he's now known. He wrote, "It means that life itself is sacred, and our duty is to cherish it." Schweitzer believed that too many people go through life without ever thinking about its meaning and value. He viewed life as a great gift that needed to be treasured and respected. Then, he said, we can raise it to its true value.

Based on the writings of both Schweitzer and those who studied him, reverence for life might best be summarized as a deep love and appreciation for:

- Life itself
- God, and the spiritual nature of mankind
- Other people, and the desire to serve them
- All living things
- Beauty in the world of nature

- The mysteries of life we'll never understand
- Honesty and integrity in all things

Schweitzer's philosophy—his deep respect—is the foundation upon which truly good people build their lives. They accept and cherish life as the great gift that it is. They treasure the world and the other people with whom they share it. The more a person does this, Schweitzer says, the more life ". . . becomes richer, more beautiful and happier. It becomes, instead of mere living, a real experience of life."

THE FOUR PILLARS OF RESPECT

Before discussing these four pillars, I want to remind my readers of something I said in the introduction. Much of what's in this book is old. Respect is as old as life itself. But I'm not alone in my belief that it's deteriorated enormously in our society during the past twenty years. Sociologists tell us it's because we've become too wrapped up in ourselves. We're into our own thing; we look out for Number One. We don't have time to give others the consideration which was once considered normal. That's now the exception. Yet, respect is still the most important quality a human being can have. And it'll always be the primary source from which the good things in life flow.

In the previous chapter I said that it's one thing to be thankful and quite another to express it. It's different with respect. *Showing* our respect is the only proof there is that we have it. Since the beginning of time, the world's most successful people have shown their respect in four ways. They're the pillars of a reverence for life.

1. Manners

Without good manners human society becomes intolerable and impossible.

GEORGE BERNARD SHAW

Call them anything you want—courtesy, respect, politeness, kindness, consideration, etiquette, thoughtfulness, graciousness, etc.—our manners are who we are. We'll always be known by the way we treat others. And the way we treat others will always be a key factor in determining how successful we become. Tom Peters and Robert Waterman, in their famous book *In Search of Excellence,* write, "Treat people as adults. Treat them as partners; treat them with dignity; treat them with respect." That's great advice for the business world; it's also great advice for everyday living. In the history of the world, no one ever went wrong by being polite.

In the 1700s Edmund Burke, a British statesman, said, "Manners are of more importance than laws." In other words, if all of us showed respect and consideration for others, we wouldn't need laws to regulate our behavior. Life is better when we treat each other with respect. More recent commentary on manners comes from public-relations expert Henry C. Rogers in 1984. He says, "If manners were an animal, it would be an endangered species."

Unfortunately, Rogers' comment has a sad ring of truth. He says he's astounded that more people don't seem to understand the importance of treating others with respect: "I simply can't comprehend how everyone doesn't see that good manners are one of the most important keys to success. . . ." And the truth is that there *has* been a decline in good manners in recent years. This is as true of adults as it is of kids. Somehow, being cool has become more important than being courteous. Whether we like to admit it or not, we *do* try to impress others. But what many people don't recognize is that the best way we can leave a good impression with others is to treat them the way we'd like them to treat us: with respect and dignity. The world's a better place, and we're better people when we have good manners.

2. Language

A man's words will always express what has been treasured in his heart.

LUKE 6:45

It's virtually impossible to conceal who we are. Our words will eventually reveal what's stored both in our hearts and in our minds. While we're not always aware of it, we say something about ourselves every time we open our mouths. The wise Solomon wrote thousands of years ago that only gracious words come from the mouths of wise people, and that fools are consumed by their own lips. We'd all be wise to examine more closely what our words are uncovering about us.

When I taught courses in communication, whether in high school or in college, I did a simple activity with my students which seemed to have quite an impact. I asked them, as a group, to identify ways in which we verbally communicate and to divide them into categories of positive and negative. They usually ended up looking like this:

Positive	*Negative*
Praise	Put-downs
Sincere compliments	Swearing
Encouragement	Biting sarcasm
Thanks	Name-calling
Truth/honesty	Laughing *at*
Belief/trust	Complaining
Sympathy	Gossip/rumor
Humor/laughing *with*	Yelling
Advice/instruction	Insincere flattery
Sharing of good news	Racial and sexual insults
Greetings	Lying/manipulating
Support	Blaming

Then I asked them this question: "Which do you hear the most frequently?" Unfortunately, the answer was the same in every class I taught. They heard more negatives than they did positives. Most of them also admitted that more negatives came out of their own mouths than did positives. Why? For the same reason that we complain more than we thank. We focus on the wrong side of life.

It took me a long time to learn the importance of gracious language. When I started working on improving my own, I began to notice that the people I most admired consistently used words that were positive and pleasant to hear. Good people are sensitive enough to choose their words carefully. What comes out of our mouths does, indeed, reveal what's stored in our hearts.

3. Honoring the rules

When . . . we, as individuals, obey laws that direct us to behave for the welfare of the community as a whole, we are indirectly helping to promote the pursuit of happiness by our fellow human beings.

ARISTOTLE

Imagine, for a minute, what a professional football game would be like if there were no rules. Chaos? Mayhem? Or worse yet, what if there *were* rules, but only one of the two teams had to obey them? How would you feel if your team was obeying the rules, and the other team wasn't? Treated unfairly? Cheated? Of course you would. We have rules and laws in order to establish some sense of fairness. Wouldn't our society be chaotic without them? Several years ago when I was teaching American Government, the textbook I used defined rules and laws as "regulations for human relations." That's really the only reason we have them—to help us be more considerate of one another.

After a presentation I did several years ago, a woman told me, "I liked everything you said except the part about obeying the rules." I asked her what her objection was. She said we had too many rules; that they were restricting. She added that they had nothing to do with being successful. I asked her if we were playing tennis against each other, would she want me to obey the rules. I asked her if she put money in a bank, would she want the bank employees to obey the laws. I asked her if she were driving her car, would she want the other drivers to obey the traffic regulations. My point was that obeying the rules or laws of our society is nothing more than showing consideration and respect for the rights of others. It's a form of honesty. What do we call people who don't play by the rules? Liars, cheats, thieves, criminals.

I often hear people say, "Rules are made to be broken" and "Everybody's doing it." At the risk of sounding like a prude or a Goody Two-shoes, I don't agree with either of those remarks. Rules aren't made to be broken; they're made to be honored. And *everybody* doesn't break the rules; it's just that the ones who do get more publicity. It's not what we can get away with that counts. It's how much consideration we show for others. Obeying the rules means we want to play fair. It also means that life will be simpler and more peaceful. Finally, it *does* have something to do with success. The people who succeed in life are the ones who show respect in all its forms.

4. Appreciating differences

The truth never becomes clear as long as we assume that each one of us, individually, is the center of the universe.

THOMAS MERTON

Not long ago, I heard a sermon about the dangers of judging others. It made sense, not only from a spiritual standpoint but also from a psychological one. I felt more than a little guilty afterward as I began to recount all the times I've judged others throughout the various stages of my life. Then, when I asked myself if it was something I still did, I felt even worse because the answer was YES. The truth is most people *do* have a problem with judging others. Since hearing that sermon, I've asked literally hundreds of people, of all ages and both in and out of church settings, if they struggle with judging others. Without a single exception, they all indicated that it's a battle for them. Some of the wiser ones told me they don't do it as much as they used to but that it was a problem they had to overcome.

So, there was some solace in knowing that I'm not alone in

this weakness, but it didn't make it OK. I recalled reading that this was one of the habits Benjamin Franklin changed after designing his famous experiment in self-improvement. He vowed to look for the good in others instead of finding fault with them, and to say only kind things about people. He said this change had a powerful effect on his life. He developed a more positive perspective of other people and improved his relationships at the same time. He attributed much of his success as a diplomat to these traits.

Why do most people judge others? The answer is simple but not very pleasant to admit. We're all self-centered. We look out for ourselves and too often make the mistake of confusing reality with our limited perception of it. Most of the time when we criticize other people, it's because they do things differently from what we do. What we're really saying is this: "You're not OK because you're not like me." I've heard people get downright insulting toward each other when discussing things as unimportant as rock groups or athletic teams. "How can you like that group?" is what both are thinking as they argue. In other words, "Only what I like is good."

Overcoming our self-centeredness and our narrow way of looking at life is a sign of real growth and maturity. When we do that, we begin to appreciate others more fully. Whether it's religious beliefs, political viewpoints, age, race, culture, leisure-time activities, or lifestyles, we need to realize that all of us have two things in common. We're the result of our genetic makeup and our experiences. No person has the "right" life. The more we learn to appreciate the differences and uniqueness in others, the closer we come to developing our own reverence for life.

THE REWARDS OF RESPECT

When we were little and first heard the word *respect,* it was a "should" or a "have-to." We were told to practice good manners, be fair, and show respect to others, especially older people. Why? Either because we were told to or because we'd get thumped upside the head if we didn't. Showing respect was something we *had* to do.

What I want to emphasize here are not the terrible things that will happen to you if you're rude, but the great rewards of being respectful. To name a few, these are the results of treating others the way we'd like them to treat us:

- We develop effective social skills and habits.
- We make other people feel good.
- We earn the respect of others.
- We establish good relationships.
- We are treated better by other people.
- We improve our feelings of self-worth.
- We build a solid reputation.

A famous phrase from the Bible reminds us that "we reap what we sow." More than anything else, respect reaps a rich harvest in life. What we send out has a way of returning. The Golden Rule—treating others as we'd like to be treated—is still golden. In fact, it's the best human-relations advice we've ever received. Good people build their lives on a foundation of respect.

Our rewards in life will always be in exact proportion to the amount of consideration we show toward others.

EARL NIGHTINGALE

CHAPTER 9

Honesty Is Still the Best Policy

Honesty is the best policy in international relations, interpersonal relations, labor, business, education, family, and crime control because truth is the only thing that works and the only foundation on which lasting relations can build.

RAMSEY CLARK

RESPECT IN ITS HIGHEST FORM

This is the most important chapter of the book. You can do many of the things I suggest here—have a positive attitude, form good habits, laugh, be thankful, set goals, motivate yourself, work hard, be self-disciplined, use time wisely, etc.—but you'll never be truly successful unless everything you do is undergirded with honesty and integrity. You'll never know peace of mind and you'll never enjoy feelings of self-worth unless truthfulness is deeply imbedded in your character. If you don't learn anything else from reading this book, it's my most sincere wish and most fervent prayer that you understand this great truth: honesty always was, is now, and always will be the best policy.

I don't mean to sound like one of the "fire and brimstone" preachers of the Puritan era, threatening you with the burning fires of hell if you tell a lie. But I do want to try to convince you, with all the passion I have, that honesty is the most essential ingredient of real success. In the previous chapter, I said that respect was the foundation upon which good people build their lives. The cornerstone, the first and most indispensable piece of that foundation, is honesty. It's respect in its highest form.

Why am I so impassioned about honesty? Because it took me too long to realize that honesty was the missing piece in my own search for success and personal fulfillment. I had most of the other pieces, but not the one on which they were all dependent. I wasn't a compulsive liar, an embezzler, or a thief; I just wasn't honest in all things. Like many others, I had the attitude that "everybody's doing it." So I did it, too. Somehow, being a little bit dishonest was OK. But also like others, I was kidding myself. I made the slow and painful discovery that there's no such thing as being a little bit dishonest. It was then that I made a conscious decision to be as honorable as I could in all things. It was a life-changing choice, one I wish I would have made much earlier. But at least I had several more years in which to experience the richness of an honest life. Some people never do. That's why if I could pass on only one thing to my own sons and other young people, it would be this: If you genuinely want to succeed in life, honesty isn't just the *best* policy; it's the *only* policy.

THE MEANING OF INTEGRITY

The key to being or becoming an honest person lies in understanding the meaning of integrity and its relationship to honesty. The two words are often used interchangeably, but *integrity* is a broader term. In regard to human nature, it means being complete. It comes from the word *integral,* which means "whole or undivided." It's defined in Merriam-Webster's New Collegiate Dictionary, Ninth Edition, as "essential to completeness." To have integrity is to be a complete person—honest and with consistently high moral standards. To live without integrity is to be an incomplete human being. Dishonesty retards both our personal and social development. It causes us to fall short of realizing our full potential for lives with inner peace, feelings of self-worth, and healthy relationships.

Schweitzer wrote that we can't have "reverence for life" unless we develop a personal code of ethics which includes honesty and truthfulness in all our dealings with other people. He says only after we develop this kind of integrity can we "feel at home in this world" and be truly effective in it. Honesty, in Schweitzer's view, is the most basic element in the personalities of people who have a genuine respect for life.

WHY HONESTY IS SUCH A STRUGGLE

One of the most honest persons I've ever known recently said to me, "I struggle with honesty every day of my life." I was both surprised and curious at his remark, so we ended up having a long talk about it. I went away from that discussion realizing that all of us are caught in a battle between right and wrong, good and evil. They're life forces that have been around since the beginning of time, and it's impossible to escape being in the middle. That's exactly where we were placed, and we're choosing between them every day.

Sadly, we're surrounded by all forms of dishonesty. Even more sad is seeing that what we can "get away with" has practically become a sport. Being able to "pull off" something is often considered an achievement, a feat worth openly bragging about. Only the dumb or unlucky ones get caught. "Everybody's doing it" is both the rallying cry and the justification for this type of behavior. To reinforce it, there are a number of movies and TV programs which seem to glorify deceit and deception. They virtually exalt them to fine arts. To top it all off, the advertising world bombards us daily with not-so-subtle messages that we should be someone other than our real selves in order to make a good impression on others.

Another reason we all struggle with honesty is that it's hard work. It requires more time, thought, and energy than we're sometimes willing to expend. Every day, we get a steady barrage of messages that we deserve things, we should have them now, and there's a quick and easy way to get them. So we often choose expediency over integrity. Why slave away on an assignment when it's easier and faster to copy someone else's? Why follow all the rules in a business transaction when a little fudging here and there can close the deal quicker and bring a bigger profit? We not only buy into the "everybody's doing it" mentality but also develop a shortcut philosophy of life. Without realizing it, we become morally lazy. It's easier and quicker to be dishonest. Is it any wonder that my friend and all the rest of us have such a struggle with honesty?

THE COST OF DISHONESTY

In the introduction I said that this is a book about what's good in people and about their potential for rich and rewarding lives. For the most part, I've tried to focus on the rewards of doing the right thing rather than on the negative outcomes of the opposite type of behavior. However, this is one case in which I feel a need to explain some of the consequences of doing the *wrong* thing. I feel this need because most people don't fully understand just how insidious dishonesty is. I was one of them for many years, and want to share here what I've learned about the destructive power it can have in our lives.

Dishonesty, more than anything else, prevents us from

being the type of persons we can and want to be. It's like a cancer. It starts small, and if not detected and completely eradicated, it spreads out of control until it finally destroys us. Yes, I really do feel that strongly about it. I've seen it cripple and ruin more lives than any disease known to mankind.

The great psychologist/philosopher William James wrote that we create our own hell in this world. He said we do it ". . . by habitually fashioning our characters in the wrong way." Lewis Andrews, a contemporary psychologist who draws upon the teachings of the great philosophers, agrees with James. In his book *To Thine Own Self Be True,* he explains his theory that dishonest behavior is at the root of most of our psychological problems. He suggests that we take ". . . a serious look at the relationship between one's values and one's health." Dishonesty is costly. These are some of the effects it can have on us.

Dishonesty is a vicious circle.

One dishonest act leads to another. Rarely does a person lie, cheat, or steal one time. If something is gained from it, the temptation to do it again is almost irresistible. Then there's a need to cover the trail, and another dishonest act is used to do it. If the process continues, dishonesty becomes almost a way of life. In other words, a habit—the worst one of all.

Dishonesty turns us into phonies and manipulators.

In St. Augustine's famous *Confessions,* written almost sixteen hundred years ago, he explains how he moved up the social ladder by deceiving and manipulating others. One day while on his way to give a speech that included several lies, he saw a beggar. He wondered why he was so discontented and this man with nothing was so cheerful. Then he realized that the beggar was authentic, true to himself; the great scholar Augustine was not. He said it helped him realize how "utterly wretched" he had become as a result of his constant phoniness. If we play a role for too long, we lose ourselves in it.

Dishonesty eventually catches up with us.

I firmly believe that we never "get away" with our dishonest acts, even though we often think we do. There may be a number of occasions on which we don't get caught, but somewhere down the road we're going to pay the price in one way or another. The ancient Chinese told us that life has a way of always balancing out, and in modern times we say "what goes around comes around." It does. Dishonesty is a path down a dingy back alley that leads to a dead end. It just takes some longer than others to realize where they're headed.

Dishonesty can't be hidden.

Isn't it true that we usually know when someone is lying to us? People tip themselves off. Their words say one thing, but their bodies say another. And we pick up the signals. The same must be true when *we* lie. Other people are picking up the same signals. We're fooling no one but ourselves. We trip over our own lies. In the process, we damage our reputations and destroy our credibility.

Dishonesty ruins relationships.

When we lie to other people, we make it hard for them to believe us in the future. Question marks start appearing after everything we say. Violating the trust of another person is a sure way of damaging a relationship. And it's more difficult to restore one than it is to form one. Without trust, good relationships are impossible.

Dishonesty attacks our nervous systems.

Quoting again from *To Thine Own Self Be True,* Dr. Andrews says that deceit has a "powerful psychological effect" on us. He says it hit home with him when he was advised by a mentor to become aware of his "insides" the next time he was tempted to lie. He adds, "The manipulative part of us is literally assaulting our vital center. . . ." He also describes research conducted at Southern Methodist University which ". . . found evidence to suggest that the effort required to sustain a false intention places an enormous stress on the body's nervous systems." We literally stir up inner turmoil when we're dishonest. In essence, we punish ourselves.

Dishonesty prevents us from fulfillment.

One of the most rewarding things in life is to discover our potential for personal fulfillment, and then grow into it. But we can't do this if we get into dishonest habits. They become roadblocks to our growth and development. If we're selfish and dishonest, we prevent ourselves from knowing what it feels like to be complete. We can never experience the satisfaction of being authentic human beings. This is the worst punishment of all.

SIX REASONS FOR BEING HONEST

While we need to see the ways in which dishonesty can ruin our lives, we also need to understand what happens when we conquer it. People who have integrity experience life at a different level. It's richer, more meaningful, and more rewarding. These are some of the ways:

1. *Peace of mind*—If someone asked me what I would do differently if I had the opportunity to live over again, my answer would be: I'd be honest in all things. I look back over my life occasionally with a certain degree of shame and embarrassment at some of the dishonest things I've said and done. It took me too long to realize that dishonesty is self-centeredness at its worst. When I finally wised up, I couldn't believe the change that took place. Since making a commitment to be honest, I've known an inner peace that I would have thought impossible. Honesty has a built-in reward: a mind at peace with itself. If there were no other reasons to be honest, this alone would be enough.

2. *Character and reputation*—Earlier in the book I said that habits are the key to success. They're also the building blocks of character and reputation, and no habit can shape them as

much as honesty. It's one of the most admired of all human traits, and it always shows through. In fact, it shines like a beacon. Good people live in the light of it.

3. *Relationships*—If dishonesty ruins relationships, honesty cements them together. The most essential ingredient of a good relationship is trust. This is true in all areas of life— friendship, marriage, family, business, education, or religion. Honesty and trust create a climate in which good relationships can develop and grow.

4. *Wholeness*—The great psychologist Carl Jung said that our deepest desire is for "wholeness." I take that to mean reaching our potential as humans, becoming the type of persons we're capable of being. Until we satisfy this desire, we'll always feel an emptiness at the very core of our existence. The only way we can fill it is with integrity. It's what makes us complete.

5. *Mental and physical health*—If dishonesty is at the root of many of our psychological problems, then honesty is a source of mental health. If dishonesty attacks our nervous systems, then honesty must strengthen them. When we're honest, we free ourselves from guilt, worry, and other forms of inner turmoil. We begin to enjoy feelings of self-respect and confidence.

There's a feeling of assurance that comes from doing the right things, from living as complete human beings. Simply put, we feel better when we're honest.

6. *Being authentic*

> *This above all, to thine own self be true,*
> *And it must follow, as the night the day,*
> *Thou canst not then be false to any man.*
>
> SHAKESPEARE

If Shakespeare hadn't chosen writing as a profession, he probably would have become one of history's greatest psychologists/philosophers. It was his keen insight into human behavior that made his writing so powerful. In the famous verse above he's simply telling us to be authentic, to be real persons instead of the fake ones we're so often tempted to be. Honesty is a choice. When we make that choice, not in a particular set of circumstances, but as a way of life, we begin to understand what it means to be an authentic person. We become what we were meant to be. Something happens inside of us, but we can't explain it to anyone else. We just feel something unbelievably good, and we begin to respect ourselves more than ever before. That's what it means to be true to ourselves. And because it feels so good to be authentic, it necessarily follows that we'll be true to others.

I said at the beginning of this chapter that it was the most important one in the book. It was also the most difficult to write. When you feel as strongly as I do about integrity, it's virtually impossible to find the right words to convey it. I can only hope that this message about honesty has the impact on your life that it had on mine. We need to be honest, not because of what might happen to us when we're not, but because of what happens inside of us when we are.

There is only one way to cope with life, namely, to find that system of values which is not subject to fashionable trends, . . . which will never change, and will always bear good fruit in terms of bringing us peace and health and assurance, even in the midst of a very insecure world.

DR. THOMAS HORA

CHAPTER 10

Kind Words Cost Little but Accomplish Much

Few things in the world are more powerful than a positive push. A smile. A word of optimism and hope. A "you can do it" when things are tough.

RICHARD M. DEVOS

A TALE OF TWO FRIENDS

When I started my teaching career at age twenty-five, a colleague who was about eight years older "took me under his wing." I felt honored because he was an outstanding teacher, and I knew I could learn a lot from him. He took the time to point out the things I was doing wrong and explained what some of my students didn't like about me. I always appreciated his criticism and worked hard to improve in these areas. As we became friends, he also gave me advice regarding my personal life. Here, also, he pointed out things I was doing wrong. Again, I appreciated his criticism. It was nice to have a friend who was willing to be so honest. There were a number of areas in which I needed to improve, both professionally and personally, and I was glad to have someone point them out. Whenever I got off track, which seemed often, he was there to show me how I'd done it. Sometimes I wondered if I'd ever become the teacher or the person that I wanted to be. But at least I always had someone to show me where I was going wrong.

As I began the sixth year of my career, our faculty was joined by Tim Hansel, who had transferred from another school. It was obvious from the first day that he was immensely popular with the students. Still learning myself, I wanted to see what his magic was. Since we were teaching the same two subjects and became team teachers in one of them, we had daily contact. It didn't take long to find out why Tim was so effective and so well liked. He seemed to have a special talent for bringing out the best in other people. With his students, instead of emphasizing their mistakes, he emphasized either what they did right or what they *could* do. In each of his classes he consistently did three things: he greeted the students as they entered the room, he praised them for their achievements, and he constantly encouraged them to be their best.

But it didn't stop there. Tim always had something good to say to me, too. He pointed out all the things I was doing well. He said he admired me for my dedication and that it was obvious that my hard work was paying off. He reminded me often how much my students liked me and how much they were learning because of my teaching. As we began to spend time together outside of school, he found other things to compliment me about. The effect of all this was that he helped me see some things that had never gotten my attention before: what I was doing *right* both as a teacher and as a person.

What became of these two friendships? Sadly, the first one ended after many years. I say *sadly* because this is a person I'd greatly admired. He had a distinguished teaching career and is a man of integrity. Most of his criticism of me was valid, and I learned a great deal from him. But one of the main reasons it ended was that the criticism was so constant. It was never balanced with any form of praise, and eventually it wore me down. The other friendship continues to flourish after thirty years. In fact, it grows richer as we grow older. I can still count on Tim to give me a lift whether I need one or not. He still reminds me about what's good in the world and what's good in me. I've known only a few people who've had as positive an effect on my life. He still has that special talent for bringing out the best in other people. Fortunately, it includes me.

The Best of All Skills

Tim has mastered a powerful skill—the ability to affirm others. *Affirm,* in my opinion, is the most powerful word in our language. It means looking for and finding good in people. It means building others up and encouraging them. It means finding reasons for praise and applause. It means nurturing and being supportive. It means reinforcing what others do well. Most of all, it means giving people reasons to celebrate.

Richard DeVos, the enthusiastic founder of the Amway Corporation, is quoted at the beginning of this chapter. He says that few things have as much power as a "positive push." I love that phrase! And I agree that there are few things in life with more power for good. When we do something well and are acknowledged for it, we're stimulated to do even better the next time. Sincere praise brings out the best in us.

The sad thing is that not enough people realize how much good can be accomplished when they affirm others. Instead of positive pushes, we get negative shoves. That's because we live in a society that seems determined to focus on what's wrong instead of what's right. More than fifty years ago, Dale Carnegie said, "Any fool can criticize, condemn, and complain—and most fools do." It's too bad that his statement still rings true today.

But keep in mind that back in Chapter 5, I urged you to think for yourself and not to let the world squeeze you into its mold. And in Chapter 6, I suggested that we can form new habits. We can train ourselves to look for the good in others and to find reasons for praising them. We bring about one of those unique situations in which everybody wins because it's impossible to make another person feel good without doing the same to yourself. As Charles Fillmore said, "We increase whatever we praise. The whole creation responds to praise, and is glad." Affirming others is the most valuable skill a person can have. It's easy, it's fun, and it gets fantastic results! And the more we do it, the better we get at it.

LESSONS FROM LINCOLN AND FRANKLIN

As a history major in college, I read the biographies of many famous Americans. That reading turned out to be the most treasured learning experience of my many years as a student. Studying the lives of great people was the best way to learn history, and it proved valuable later when I began studying the psychology of success. In fact, it was the reading of those biographies which led to my interest in psychology. Nothing helps us understand the meaning of success better than reading about people who made the most of their lives.

Two of those famous people were Abraham Lincoln and Benjamin Franklin. One is best known as a great president who ended slavery; the other as a distinguished scholar, inventor, and statesman. But it wasn't their claims to fame which interested me the most. It was how each of these men became experts in human relations and in the art of affirming others. Their greatest trait was the ability to get along with all types of people and to bring out the best in them. In fact, it was this skill more than any other which made them as successful as they were.

My favorite history teacher in college absolutely loved Abraham Lincoln and seemed to know everything about him. His name just happened to be Dr. Ashbrook Lincoln, and, of course, he signed his name "A. Lincoln." I can still vividly recall a series of lectures he gave about the genius of President Lincoln. He said Lincoln's greatness was in his ability to deal successfully with others. I was fascinated by the descriptions of the diverse people who surrounded him in the White House. They all had two things in common: enormous talent and an ego to match. They also thought they were superior to the President. But instead of getting rid of them, Lincoln honored them. He praised their abilities, sought their advice, and encouraged them to devote their talents and energy to serving the country. And everyone came out a winner.

Franklin is often portrayed as a natural diplomat, a man born with a personality that was pleasing to others. But that's far from the truth. By Franklin's own admission, he had several personality flaws, and it was through hard work and diligence that he perfected the human-relations skills which ultimately led to his great diplomatic achievements. In his autobiography Franklin tells about how difficult it was to overcome his natural inclination to judge and criticize others. He called his attempt to improve himself a "bold and arduous project." But his plan worked, and he eventually formed new habits. He trained himself to look for the positive characteristics of others and then resolved to speak ". . . all the good I know of everybody."

Lincoln and Franklin had both discovered one of the keys to succeeding in life: affirming others. They understood the great power of the double-win principle and worked hard at helping bring out the best in others. In lifting others, they lifted themselves to honored places in history.

WHAT'S GOOD ABOUT ME

When I taught psychology courses, we did an exercise in affirming others. It was a simple activity, yet one of the most effective teaching techniques I ever used. We arranged the desks in a semicircle facing a single chair called the "hot seat," which each student took a turn in. In the first part of the exercise, the one in the hot seat was asked to tell the rest of us "What's good about me." Obviously, this wasn't easy, but it was an important part of the unit on affirmation. I wanted my students to learn to affirm *themselves* also—to be able to acknowledge their positive characteristics and habits. It usually took them about two minutes to do this first part. They had a hard time telling others what they liked about themselves. In the second part, the students in the semicircle told the one in the hot seat what he or she left out. The only rule was that the comments couldn't be about looks or clothing. The person in the hot seat then listened to compliments and praise for several minutes.

To say that this exercise had a positive effect would be a great understatement. It had a powerful effect on every person in the room. When we discussed it the next day, the students were still beaming. They talked about how great it felt, not only to hear good things about themselves but also to learn more about what they were doing right. It encouraged them to build on their strengths, and it increased both their confidence and their self-esteem. I asked them to write down the things they learned from the unit on affirmation in general and from this exercise in particular. Over the years, I received hundreds of great responses. The ones that came up most often were these:

- There's a lot more good in people than there is bad.
- We need to get in the habit of looking for what's good in others.
- Building people up is more effective than tearing them down.
- Nothing feels better than genuine praise from others.
- We all need recognition and encouragement.
- It feels good to make someone else feel good.
- Affirmation brings out the best in people—everybody wins!

I can't think of a better way to conclude this chapter. An encouraging word really does go a long way—further than you ever dreamed possible.

Kind words do not cost much. . . . Yet they accomplish much.

BLAISE PASCAL

CHAPTER 11

Real Motivation Comes from Within

No matter who you are or what your age may be, if you want to achieve permanent, sustaining success, the motivation that will drive you toward that goal must come from within.

PAUL J. MEYER

WHAT IS MOTIVATION, AND WHERE DOES IT COME FROM?

I'm frequently asked to give motivational talks to educators, parents, students, businesses, conferences, etc. I generally accept those invitations, but not until first clarifying an important point with the program director. I explain that I don't really give motivational speeches because I don't believe in them. I know that a lot of highly paid motivational gurus around the country might disagree with me, but I don't think one person can motivate another. I do believe, though, that one person can help another understand what motivation is and where it comes from. I also believe that one person can teach another the key ingredients of self-motivation, which is the only real kind. Most importantly, I believe that one person can help another stay motivated by giving needed encouragement, just as the friend I described in the previous chapter does for me. As a teacher, speaker, and writer, these are the three things I try to do.

Motivation is a highly misunderstood concept. Many people, when they hear the word, think of legendary football coaches like Notre Dame's Knute Rockne telling his team to "win one for the Gipper," or Vince Lombardi telling his Green Bay Packers that "the will to win is everything." But that isn't motivation; it's temporary stimulation. It's great in sports and in other ventures that require short bursts of energy, but it doesn't work in everyday life. Unless, of course, you can find someone to walk around with you all day yelling, "Go, go, go! Win, win, win!"

That's why I said I didn't believe in motivational speeches. Maybe I'm just not the "rah-rah" type, but that approach has always seemed short-lived and shallow to me. It can be highly entertaining and can tug at our emotions, but the motivation leaves with the speaker. It's the same with writing. I don't believe in making wild promises like "you can have it all" or "you can be anything." I think people want and need something with more depth and sincerity. They want something that lasts longer and helps them deal with life as it really is. So instead of trying to motivate people, I try to teach them *about* motivation and how they can motivate themselves.

There are countless theories on motivation. Psychologists have never been able to agree on why some people are motivated and others aren't. And every parent, teacher, and employer in the world wishes they'd find out. But we don't need to concern ourselves with all of the mysteries about motivation. We only need to know two things about it. The first is found back in Chapter 1, where I wrote that successful people accept responsibility for their own lives. That means they don't wait for someone else to motivate them; they do it themselves. The second thing we need to understand is the origin of the word *motivation*. It comes from *motive*, which Webster's defines as "that within the individual, rather than without, which causes him or her to act." In other words, all of our actions have motives, or reasons. They come from needs felt deeply inside. And no one else can fill them for us.

Yet, we live in a society that tries to convince us of just the opposite. It seems as if someone is always there with an inspiring message telling us what we need to have or what we need to do. But that kind of stimulus is both external and temporary, and more than likely phony. It isn't real motivation because it doesn't come from us. Remember back in Chapter 5 when I said we need to think for ourselves? Well, an important part of that thinking includes motivation. When it's internal and deeply rooted, it can propel us to achievements beyond anything we ever thought possible.

THE THREE KEYS TO MOTIVATING YOURSELF

Think for a moment about an important goal you have—something you're certain you want to achieve in life. Now check your motivation by answering these three questions:

- Do you have enough desire to attain it?
- Do you have a real belief that you can accomplish it?
- Do you have a clear mental picture of yourself achieving it?

If your answer to all three is a confident YES, then you're ready. Because these are the keys to being self-motivated.

1. Desire

Motivation starts with a sense of desire. . . . When you want something, you become motivated to get it.

DENIS WAITLEY

Desire is the seed from which all achievement grows. More than any other characteristic, it determines whether we're going to be mediocre or successful in life. Desire, not ability, separates average people from those who excel. It's that something extra which makes it possible for ordinary people to accomplish extraordinary things. I love the old phrase "burning desire" because it's so descriptive. People who have it are almost impossible to stop. The stronger the flame burns, the greater the determination, and the more likely the success.

A good example of this was Barbara, a woman in one of my university classes. Like many in this particular program, she returned to college after a long absence. In her mid-forties, she wanted to complete the degree she'd started working on at age eighteen. Understandably, she was a bit intimidated at first. I remember her saying that she just wanted her bachelor's degree and would be more than happy if she could earn a B average. I noticed after only a week that she had a real passion burning inside, not just to learn but to excel. Her first set of assignments was so outstanding, I suggested that she might want to set her sights a bit higher. She beamed! She also continued to produce work of the highest quality. I remember writing on one of her papers, "You are absolutely on fire! What a joy it is to be part of your learning." Desire can be contagious, and when the flame gets fanned a little, some amazing things can happen. Hers was burning brightly, and she elevated her goals to an A average and a master's degree, both of which she went on to earn.

An important aspect of desire is commitment—a promise that we make to no one but ourselves. This is what keeps us going when things are the toughest. Instead of giving up in the face of adversity or defeat, we bounce back. Famous psychologist Dr. Joyce Brothers thinks commitment is the pivotal quality of success. She says, "Total commitment is the common denominator among successful men and women. Its importance cannot be overestimated." This kind of desire has a way of strengthening us. It helps us make sacrifices when they're needed, and it helps us dig down for extra effort in seeing our goals through to completion. Desire is a powerful inner force—one of the key ingredients of success.

2. Belief

Your chances of success in any undertaking can always be measured by your belief in yourself.

ROBERT COLLIER

Several years ago I discovered that a large percentage of my students were being crippled by a disease. It was preventing them from living as human beings were meant to live. It was both deadly and highly contagious, as it had spread all over the school. One of the strangest things about it was that hardly any of them knew they had it. In fact, it didn't even have a name. So I gave it one. I told them that there was an epidemic of EFWIC disease going around. They responded by giving me puzzled looks and a chorus of "huhs?"

I told them EFWIC meant "excuses for why I can't." More puzzled looks. I rolled out about six feet of butcher paper and tacked it next to the door. Then I said, "Every time you catch yourself making an excuse today, or hear anyone else making one, I want you to write it down. Tomorrow when you come in here, write all your excuses on this paper, which we'll call the Master Excuse List." It got filled up so fast the next morning that we had to use another sheet that was about two feet longer. By the end of the week we had a wall covered with excuses for why people thought they couldn't do things. I asked them if anyone could explain why I considered habitual excuse-making a disease. The quietest kid in the class raised his hand for the first time all semester. He said, "If we're always looking for excuses for why we *can't* do things, we'll never find the reasons why we *can*." I held up my arms and exclaimed, "Hallelujah! Those are as good as any 'words to live by' that I've ever heard."

We *do* need to look for more reasons why we can instead of why we can't. The only limitations we have are the ones put on us, first by others and then by ourselves. They exist because we believe them, and they won't disappear until we exchange them for a new set of beliefs. In the introduction of this book, I wrote that most people don't know how good they are and how much they can accomplish with their lives. We need to realize that we're more capable than we give ourselves credit for. We have inner resources we've never used. But remember, that's good news. The first step to tapping into all that potential is to increase our belief in ourselves at least enough to try, even to risk failure. Eventually, this effort pays off. It leads to small achievements and builds self-confidence. This, in turn, brings more success. As habits of constructive thinking take over, a new cycle is set in motion. We believe in ourselves, and we start looking for reasons why we *can*.

Richard DeVos, a successful businessman and the author of *BELIEVE!,* says he's frequently asked for his secrets about motivation. But he claims that he doesn't know anything about motivation and that he has no secrets, tricks, or gimmicks. He says the most valuable thing he's ever learned is that most people can accomplish whatever they believe they can: "More than any other single lesson, my experiences have conspired to teach me the value of determined, confident effort. . . . Believe you can, and you'll find out that you can! Try! You'll be surprised at how many good things can happen."

Good things happen because when we believe, we *make* them happen.

3. Mental picture

You must first clearly see a thing in your mind before you can do it.

ALEX MORRISON

In the early 1930s an engineer named Joseph Strauss went often to a location in San Francisco where he could view the opening of the bay. In his mind he formed a picture of a beautiful bridge connecting the two sides. The more he thought about it, the clearer the picture became. In 2002 we celebrated the sixty-fifth anniversary of his dream, the Golden Gate Bridge.

In 1961 President John Kennedy said we should make it our goal to put a man on the moon and return him safely to earth before the decade was over. Millions of people thought that was impossible, but a determined group of workers at NASA already had clear pictures in their minds of it happening. When we watched Neil Armstrong walk on the moon and return to earth in 1969, they'd already seen it thousands of times.

When Bill Gates was an undergraduate at Harvard, the personal computer was still in its early stages of development. Most people saw it as a machine to be used for storing large amounts of data and for word processing. Gates saw other possibilities. He envisioned then many of the things we do with our computers today. He thought about them often while attending lectures on subjects in which he wasn't particularly interested. Not only did he think about them, but he also began to visualize the software that would revolutionize the way we live. Pictures in his mind turned into drawings on paper. We know the rest of the story.

Tiger Woods is one of many world-class athletes who form vivid mental images to prepare themselves for competition. He explains some of the techniques he's developed in his 2001 book, *How I Play Golf.* He talks about "the game within the game" and how important it is to master the mental aspect of any sport. Before the Master's tournament he watches videos of both himself and others who've won. This helps him both "see" and "feel" the course before he even arrives in Augusta. He also claims that "instant recall of past successes" helps him prepare for a particular shot. In his mind's eye he watches himself succeed before he actually does it physically.

The technique used in the four examples described previously is known by different names: visualization, mental rehearsal, guided imagery. I call it forming a mental picture. Keep in mind that we don't think in words; we think in pictures. The more clearly and more often we picture ourselves doing something, the more likely we are to do it. It all starts in the mind. Our images are great motivators.

Dr. Charles Garfield, a psychologist at the University of California, has specialized for years in studying the habits of high achievers in science, business, industry, and athletics. He wrote about many of them in his book *Peak Performers*. He says there's something all of them do: they ". . . report a highly developed ability to imprint images of successful actions in the mind. They practice, mentally, specific skills and behaviors leading to those outcomes and achievements which they ultimately attain." Garfield also reports on something which they believe: "All maintain that the potential for major increases in achievement and self-development exists in everyone, and that the starting point is an internal decision to excel."

If you have a burning desire, a solid belief, and a clear picture, you have all the motivation you'll ever need.

Motivation is an inner drive.

DENIS WAITLEY

CHAPTER 12

Goals Are Dreams
with Deadlines

---

*People with goals succeed because they know where
they're going.*

EARL NIGHTINGALE

MOTIVATION AND GOALS:
A POWERFUL COMBINATION

There's a good reason why the chapter on goals follows the
one on motivation. Together, they're not only the greatest
source of human power but the seed of all success. When we
combine motivation with our goals, there's hardly anything
that can stop us. All achievements, no matter how great or
small, are ignited as goals and fueled through motivation.

In the last chapter, I said I was often asked to give motivational speeches. While I don't believe in them, I *do* accept most of the invitations. Does that sound like a contradiction? It isn't. Rather than try to motivate people, I speak on the importance of self-motivation and explain the roles of desire, belief, and mental pictures. Then I talk about my favorite subject: goals. There's nothing I would rather speak, write, or teach about. Goals not only encompass all of life but are the most effective self-motivators we can have. The goals we set and the depth of our motivation will determine, more than anything else, what we make of our lives.

Why Goals Are So Important

There are many ways to define success. The best definition I've ever seen is this: *Success is the progressive accomplishment of worthy goals.*

If there's one thing on which all the experts on human achievement agree, it's the importance of setting goals. Success doesn't happen by accident. It happens by design. Charles Garfield, the psychologist quoted in the previous chapter, has worked with astronauts, world-class athletes, scientists, inventors, business leaders, and other high achievers. He believes that any type of success "starts with a mission": a specific goal accompanied by strong desire. Goals have been the starting place for every advancement in the history of mankind. The process is always the same: a dream becomes a goal, the goal becomes an achievement. Or in the words of

Napoleon Hill, "What the mind of man can conceive and believe, it can achieve."

Living without goals is like going on a trip without a destination. If you don't know where you're going, you'll probably end up nowhere, and any road will get you there. Despite living in a country with unlimited opportunity, that's where millions of people end up: nowhere. Yet they don't seem to understand why. Tragically, I see too many young people headed for the same place. It's tragic because it doesn't have to be that way. There's something relatively simple that can change the course of anyone's life, regardless of age or circumstances. That something is a clearly defined set of goals.

Unfortunately, we don't learn about goals in the classroom. As great as our educational system is, it's lacking in some vital areas. That's why I said in the introduction that we don't teach "how life works" or "what is essential" in school. Goal-setting is one of those essentials. Hopefully, this chapter will fill in one of the gaps in your education. Over the past thirty years, I've seen lives (including my own) change dramatically because of goals. It's almost unbelievable what people can do when they discover what goals are, the benefits of setting them, and how to achieve them.

THE BENEFITS OF SETTING GOALS

Having goals can enrich our lives in a number of ways:

- **Motivation**—Goals are the starting blocks of motivation. They give us a reason to get off our duffs and get going.

- **Independence**—Goals help us take charge of our own lives. Instead of following the crowd or wandering through life, we choose our own path, the one that leads to fulfillment of our ambitions.

- **Direction**—Goals give us a destination. We're more likely to get someplace when we know where we're going.

- **Meaning**—Goals give us a sense of purpose. Life has more meaning when we're clear on what we want. Instead of merely existing from one day to the next, our goals give us reasons to start really living.

- **Enjoyment**—Goals are the antidote to the most dreaded of all social diseases: boredom. Goals make our lives more fun, more interesting, and more challenging.

- **Fulfillment**—Goals, more than anything else, help us reach our potential. Setting goals helps us see what's possible. Each successful step toward attaining them builds confidence. Each goal completed helps us see more of what's possible and leads to new goals and more success.

WHEN A DREAM BECOMES A GOAL

I taught a college course in organizational change and planning, which included corporate goal-setting. Since I wanted my students also to consider personal change and planning, I devoted part of the class to individual goal-setting. I gave a simple homework assignment: write down ten lifetime goals. In the following class I asked each student to share one of them. Diane, a wonderful and enthusiastic woman in her mid-forties, went first. She said, "I've always had the dream of someday living in Europe." I said, "That's great, and it's almost a goal. We can turn it into one by doing just a couple of simple things." I got puzzled looks and the question that I knew would follow: "Why isn't it a goal?" Diane wanted to know.

"Goals are dreams with deadlines," was my answer. I explained that when we put a target date on our dreams, it's the first step in turning them into goals. Next question: "What's the other thing needed to turn it into a goal?" Answer: "Europe is a big place, an entire continent. How about narrowing it down to a specific country, or better yet, a region or a city?" I went on to explain that "the dream of living in Europe someday" was a good example of a "near goal." They're dreams that usually don't become reality because they don't have enough clarity. The human mind won't move in the direction of a generality; it will move when it has something specific to aim at. A good example is the one I gave in the last chapter. The more Joseph Strauss' picture of the Golden Gate Bridge became vivid and detailed, the more he moved toward making it become a reality.

The adults in this particular class seemed especially interested in goals, so we did additional exercises, and I taught them the basic principles of setting goals and achieving them. When they completed an evaluation of the course content later, all of them said that the unit on individual goal-setting was the most valuable. Later that year they all received their college degrees, and we celebrated at a class-reunion party shortly afterward. And then we went our separate ways.

About three years later, I received an envelope with a postmark from Vienna, Austria. I opened it, and read these words across the top of the page: "GOALS ARE DREAMS WITH DEADLINES!" It was a letter from Diane. She explained that she'd changed her "someday" into a specific year and then narrowed down "Europe," first to Austria, then to Vienna. She had a wonderful job with the United Nations and had become engaged. Her dream had come true—and then some! Near the end of her letter, she said she knew that I had a long list of travel goals. "Is Vienna on the list? Have you ever been here? Is there any chance you'll be coming to Austria?" she wanted to know. My answers were "Yes, no, and yes." Vienna was on my list because I'd never been there, and it just happened to be on my itinerary for a trip planned that summer. Less than two months after receiving her letter, Diane; her fiancé; my wife, Cathy; and I had dinner together in Vienna. What a celebration!

This is a great example of what can happen when a dream becomes a goal. Think what could happen if you sat down and wrote out an entire list of goals, and then started working on them. I know exactly what would happen because I did this about thirty years ago. Those goals became the blueprint for a very rewarding life. I was about thirty when I first learned about the principles and benefits of setting goals. The goals I wrote then, and the ones I've added since, have enriched my life beyond anything I would ever have thought possible. Now in my early sixties, I have more goals than ever, and I'm having a wonderful time checking off the completed ones and adding new ones. Believe me, it's great fun!

MY BEST SUGGESTIONS

If I was granted one wish for improving education in this country, it would be to include instruction in goal-setting in every school and college. It's that important. More than anything else, goals give us direction, lead to achievement, and result in rewarding lives. I've thought about writing an entire book about goals. There's that much to say about the advantages and the benefits of having them. I've conducted all-day workshops on goal-setting and taught entire units about it, yet I never felt I'd covered everything. So, in a book of this nature, I can't give you the complete picture. However, I can give you these suggestions for getting started in goal-setting and increasing the excitement level of your life:

1. Understand the difference between a goal and a wish

Ask a hundred people what their goals are, and these are the three answers you'll get most frequently: to be happy, to be rich, to be famous. Those aren't goals; they're wishes. A wish is a vague dream that we hope happens *to* us. There's a vast difference between that and a goal. A goal is a clear picture that becomes an achievement because we *make* it happen. It requires hard work, self-discipline, and good use of time, which just happen to be the subjects of the next three chapters.

2. Write down your goals, and make them specific

We draw up plans for buildings, businesses, meetings, weddings, sports, parties, vacations, retirement, etc. But do we draw up plans for our lives? That's what goals are. One of the best investments you'll ever make is to invest some time in sitting down, thinking, and writing out a list of goals. It can become the blueprint for an exciting and rewarding life. Writing your goals down is the first act of commitment—to yourself. And seeing them on paper is the first phase of turning them into reality.

Write your goals as specifically as you can. Put deadlines on them. The more precise they are, the more your mind will be drawn to them. Here are some other things to consider while you're drawing up your life plan: What are the steps you need to take to accomplish the big goals? What are the obstacles you'll have to overcome? Whose help do you need? What do you need to learn? What will the rewards be? The more precisely you write about your goals, the clearer the picture becomes.

3. Categorize and balance your goals

One of the keys to succeeding in life is to live it with some sense of balance. Having goals in only one category puts blinders on us. It narrows our vision and makes us become one-dimensional. The best way to avoid this is to divide our goals into categories that allow us to experience some of the great varieties of life. This helps us keep things in perspective. It brings balance to our goals as well as to our lives.

The first personal goal list I saw was divided into categories, so I did the same with mine. Keep in mind that goals are not carved in stone. There's no rule that says we can't change our plans. In thirty years some of my goals, and even some of my categories, have changed as my interests and values have changed. But I'm still convinced that different categories of goals make life more interesting. Although I would encourage you to make up your own categories, you might find it helpful in getting started to see the ones I presently have:

- Education
- Career
- Income
- Own *(things I want to have)*
- Family
- Fun/Adventure *(things I want to do)*
- Athletic
- Personal growth
- Spiritual

- Learn to do
- Travel—within the United States
- Travel—foreign

4. Review and revise your goals regularly

Do you ever make a "things to do" list? Isn't it true that the more you look at the list, the more things on it get done? That's why we usually keep those kinds of lists someplace visible. It works the same way with goals. We need to "see" them often, a minimum of once a week. The words we see become the mental pictures I wrote about earlier. We become what we think about; we become our pictures. They're like previews of coming attractions. Regularly visualizing our goals is what makes us move in their direction. It helps us focus on our targets.

It's also a good idea to revise them at least once a year. I do it each January. If something I wrote down earlier is no longer a goal, instead of crossing it out, I write *NLG* in front of it. Since goal-setting is an ongoing process, it's nice to be able to look back later and see how you've changed. I also add new goals and sometimes change the categories or develop subcategories, as I did with my travel goals when I divided them into "United States" and "foreign." Another valuable thing to do in January is to mark all the goals you're going to accomplish in that calendar year.

Look at your goals frequently, revise them when needed, and most important, think about (picture) them as much as you can.

SUMMARY

Goals give us direction and purpose.
Goals add meaning to our lives.
Goals challenge us.
Goals make life more interesting.
Goals make life more rewarding.
Goals make life better.

Virtually nothing on earth can stop a person with a positive attitude who has his goal clearly in sight.
DENIS WAITL

CHAPTER 13

There's No Substitute for Hard Work

The best prize life offers is the chance to work hard at work worth doing.

THEODORE ROOSEVELT

THE REWARDS OF HARD WORK

Motivation is fantastic and goals are great, but nothing happens until hard work is added. If something is worth achieving, it's worth an all-out effort. The good things in life come to us as the result of time, energy, sacrifice, and even the risk of failure. So success requires a certain amount of toughness. It comes to people who aren't afraid of a challenge and some good, old-fashioned hard work. If we want our dreams to come true, it has to be part of the formula.

But the best thing about hard work is that it does more than make our dreams come true. It has other rewards and benefits. Here are ten of them:

1. *Hard work helps us realize our potential.* As our work begins to pay off, it stimulates us to increase our effort. It helps us see what's possible. Success brings confidence, and confidence brings more success.

2. *Hard work helps us face up to life.* Life is hard (Chapter 2). We're challenged every day to choose between whimpering about it or standing up to it. Hard work and a good attitude are the best tools we have.

3. *Hard work makes us feel good.* There's no greater feeling of satisfaction than that of completing a task and knowing that we've done our best.

4. *Hard work builds character.* There's no better measure of who we are than our willingness to work. Enduring and honest effort brings out the best in us.

5. *Hard work earns the respect of others.* We're admired when we give our best, especially when it's done consistently. We earn the confidence and trust of others. We also earn a solid reputation.

6. *Hard work earns self-respect.* Consistently giving our best also helps us develop respect for ourselves. Whether we succeed or not, we always feel better when we try.

7. *Hard work adds meaning.* Working toward our goals is one of the most meaningful and rewarding experiences in life. As long as we have a purpose, we have a good reason to get out of bed in the morning.

8. *Hard work gets the best results.* Life is more interesting and enjoyable when we're productive. Fulfillment is the result of wholehearted effort.

9. *Hard work becomes a habit.* Habits are the key to all success (Chapter 6), and the best four are honesty, politeness, hard work, and thankfulness.

10. *Hard work is healthy.* When we work hard, we use our minds and bodies in positive ways, so it induces both mental and physical health. Hard workers are healthier and live longer. Hard work is good for us.

THE COMMON DENOMINATOR OF SUCCESS

Some of the most extensive research on the subject of success was conducted by George and Alec Gallup, well known public-opinion poll-takers, and William Proctor, a reporter.

They spent more than a thousand hours interviewing people whose achievements have earned them a place in *Who's Who in America* and who have been acknowledged as successful in a wide variety of endeavors: business, science, the arts, literature, education, religion, the military, etc.

The interviews included questions about family background, education, personality, interests, abilities, religious beliefs, and personal values. The goal of the researchers was to determine what these high-achieving people had in common. Their answers varied widely in these areas, but there was one common thread: the willingness to work long, hard hours. All of them agreed that success wasn't something that had just happened to them due to luck or special talents. It happened because they'd *made* it happen through great effort and dogged determination. Instead of looking for shortcuts and ways to avoid hard work, these people welcomed it as a necessary part of the process. There was general agreement among them that the people who are truly successful are the ones who most *deserve* it. All of them have paid the price.

One of the achievers interviewed, when asked for his personal formula for success, answered, ". . . Pride in what I do but also the guts and stamina to work the hours required to accomplish the objectives." This response was representative of most. Virtually all of them placed a high premium on the willingness to work hard over a long period. They agreed that establishing good work habits (there's that word *habits* again) is the most important ingredient in any type of success.

Another goal of the authors was to answer the question "Who can be a success?" The answer is encouraging. After compiling the data from all their interviews, they came to this conclusion: "One of the lessons of this book is that anyone can be a success!" Too many people assign themselves to positions of mediocrity in life when they have the potential to be much more. Almost all can succeed in life if they're willing to take the right steps to bring it about. The three most important ones are to get motivated, to set goals, and to work hard enough to achieve them. The authors said they didn't find anything startling as a result of all their research, but they did find something that supports a time-honored belief: "So what we have here is an affirmation of the old-fashioned American credo that hard work and determination pay off."

BUT WHAT ABOUT THE SHORTCUTS?

When I was growing up in the 1950s, the message was pretty simple: Success is something you have to earn. You have to be patient because it takes a lot of hard work and sacrifice for a long time. I think the media blitzes us today with a message that's just the opposite: There's a quick and easy way to get everything we want. Recently, within a period of two days, I heard on the radio that anyone can lose fifty pounds, speak a foreign language, get a contractor's license, become a disc jockey, and earn millions in the real-estate market. Now there's no question that we *can* do all of these things if we really want to. But the main part of each message is that we don't have to work, wait, struggle, or make any sacrifice. We can do all of these things within a matter of days and without the slightest effort. Maybe Santa

Claus, the Easter Bunny, and our Fairy Godmother make them happen.

Unfortunately, if we hear things often enough, we begin to believe them. And too many people, of all ages, have bought into this phony formula for success. They've adopted a push-button mentality along with the quick-and-easy philosophy of life. They focus on consuming rather than producing. They focus on short-term pleasure rather than long-term satisfaction. And then they make the painful discovery that life doesn't work the way it's portrayed in the media. That's why I said in Chapter 5 that we have to learn to think for ourselves. There are no shortcuts, gimmicks, tricks, or secrets that lead to success. There's just hard work, and there's no substitute for it.

WORK AND FUN AREN'T OPPOSITES

The purpose of this chapter is obviously to point out the benefits of hard work. But I don't want to imply that in order to succeed in life, we have to be working all the time. That would be unhealthy for both us and the people we're close to. Remember that in Chapter 3, I emphasized the importance of laughing and having fun. In Chapter 12, I listed my goal categories. One of the biggest is called "Fun/Adventure." Believe me, I've had a ball doing many of those things and dreaming about the ones I'm still going to do.

We need to take a break from our work in order to have fun and maintain the balance that's so important in life. But we also need to understand that work and fun are not exclusive of each other. We can laugh, play, and enjoy ourselves while we're working. I think teaching is one of the hardest jobs in the world, especially if it's done right. I worked my rear end off at it for thirty-five years, but I also had a wonderful time. My high-school and college students could occasionally be a pain, but most of the time they were eager, polite, full of surprises, and fun to be with. I'm certainly not alone. I hang out only with positive people, and I know a lot of lawyers, doctors, and businessmen who also turn their work into play. Work hard, but have fun doing it.

Armand Hammer, the great industrialist who died in 1990 at the age of ninety-two, was once asked how a man his age had the energy to continually circle the globe to conduct business and meet with the heads of governments. He said, "I love my work. I can't wait to start a new day. I never wake up without being full of ideas. Everything is a challenge." George Bernard Shaw, one of the most successful playwrights of all time, said something similar about a hundred years earlier. He wrote, "I want to be thoroughly used up when I die, for the harder I work, the more I live." I think Hammer and Shaw would have agreed with me that there's no substitute for hard work.

So much unhappiness, it seems to me, is due to nerves; and bad nerves are the result of having nothing to do, or doing a thing badly, unsuccessfully, or incompetently. Of all the unhappy people in the world, the unhappiest are those who have not found something they want to do. True happiness comes to him who does his work well, followed by a relaxing and refreshing period of rest. True happiness comes from the right amount of work for the day.

LIN YÜ-T'ANG

CHAPTER 14

You Have to Give Up Something to Get Something

Decide what you want, decide what you are willing to exchange for it, establish your priorities, and go to work!

H. LAMAR HUNT

ANOTHER KEY TO ACHIEVEMENT

Motivating yourself, setting goals, and working hard will take you a long way. Add self-discipline, and you'll go even farther. It's part of the formula for personal achievement. It may be the most essential part, because every successful person I've ever known or read about says it's the absolute key to getting things done. Without it, you'll accomplish little. With it, you'll accomplish more than you ever dreamed possible.

Since I'm so big on self-discipline, it's important to clarify what it is. But because it's a term that's often misunderstood, I need to first explain what it *isn't*. Some people think self-discipline is something to be avoided because it has a negative sound to it. They confuse it with self-inflicted punishment. It's also too often thought of as self-restriction or self-denial. I heard someone say recently that people with self-discipline are rigid and inflexible. All of these notions are wrong. Real self-discipline is one of the most positive attributes a person can have. I like the way Webster's defines *discipline:* "training that corrects, molds, strengthens, or perfects." What could be more positive than that? Self-discipline means training yourself to get things done. It means developing your own plan of achievement, committing yourself to it, and then following through. Self-discipline might also be looked upon as self-determination. When you practice it, you realize that you're in control of your own life. You alone determine what you'll accomplish, and when. And you alone decide what you'll make of your life. Ultimately, self-discipline means being in charge of yourself.

My own definition of *self-discipline* is this: "getting yourself to do something, even though you don't feel like it, because the reward for getting it done far exceeds the temporary unpleasantness of the task itself." Let's say you want to get into the best possible physical condition. You can do it, but not without giving up something. It requires hard work, sacrifice, pain, and a whole lot of self-discipline. Ask any runner, swimmer, weight lifter, or triathlete if training is always enjoyable. You'll get a resounding NO for an answer. Ask if it means giving up something pleasant to do something that hurts, and the answer is YES. That seems like a pretty dumb thing to do, but there must be a reason. Is it worth all the time, pain, and sacrifice? YES! The reward is greater than what you give up, and it lasts a lot longer.

It doesn't make any difference what you want to be good at. Whether it's art, music, sports, business, computers, or tiddlywinks, you'll need to develop self-discipline. Philosopher Erich Fromm said that without self-discipline our lives become chaotic and lack concentration. If we do things only when we're in the mood, then it's no more than a hobby. He says we'll never be good at anything until we do it in a disciplined way. An important part of our personal development is learning to take responsibility for ourselves. That's what self-discipline is. It means accepting the fact that life is hard, and that nothing worthwhile ever comes easily or without a price. It means being willing to give up some temporary enjoyment in order to work at something that has a more lasting reward. It helps us better understand what Benjamin Franklin meant when he said there's no gain without pain. Self-discipline puts us in charge of both the pain and the gain. That's when real accomplishment takes place.

DELAYED GRATIFICATION: THE HEART OF SELF-DISCIPLINE

We live in a society that worships comfort, ease, pleasure, and instant gratification. Think how many things we can do just by pushing a single button: open the garage door, cook dinner, make a phone call, wash and dry the clothes, send an e-mail, turn on the TV, change the channel, warm us up, cool us down.

And these are just at home. We have more buttons in the car and at work. Push a button, get it done quickly and easily. No sweat, no strain. And then to reinforce it, we get bombarded with messages that say, "You can have it all!" "You can have it now!" "You deserve it!" Obviously, a lot of people have bought into this philosophy. I was reminded of it every time I saw that credit-card commercial that shouted, "Master the possibilities!" You see pictures of all the things you can have and all the exotic places you can go just by flashing a little piece of plastic. Play now, pay later! This is the way life works. Actually, this *is* the way life works for too many people. They look for the quick way, the easy way, and they play now. So they pay later. And, believe me, they *do* pay! That approach to life, no matter how many people get sucked into it, is backward. Real success comes when we pay now and play later. It's called self-discipline, and at the heart of it is the principle of delayed gratification: the willingness and the ability to postpone pleasure. It means the work, the pain, and the sacrifice come now, and the good things come afterward. There's no such thing as instant gratification. There's no prize without a price.

In an earlier chapter I referred to Scott Peck's wonderful book, *The Road Less Traveled.* The road he refers to is the one that has a sign at the entrance saying, "Life is difficult." Those just happen to be the first three words in the book. That's why this road is less traveled. Too many people are looking for the one *without* difficulties. They're looking for Easy Street. There isn't one. Peck says if we learn to schedule the pain and sacrifice first, and get them over with, we'll enhance the pleasure that comes later. Notice that he doesn't say *avoid* the pain; he says *schedule* it. Whatever the price is for getting something done, pay it first. You have to give up something to get something.

MAKING CHOICES:
WHAT ARE YOU WILLING TO GIVE UP?

Discipline means choices. Every time you say yes to a goal or objective, you say no to many more.

SYBIL STANTON

Three examples of choosing delayed gratification

1. My university students were mostly adults who worked full-time and had families. The program they were in was intense, to say the least. In addition to working forty or more hours at their jobs, they attended a four-hour class once a week, and were expected to put in another twenty hours doing assignments and reading. They had to make some important choices if they wanted to succeed in the program.

What they gave up: entertainment, leisure time on weekends, sleep, vacations, family outings, hobbies, a relaxing lifestyle.

What they got: knowledge, a college degree, the desire for life-long learning, an opportunity to advance at work, a sense of accomplishment, increased self-esteem, the admiration of family, friends, and colleagues.

2. In the late 1980s I was teaching a unit on the psychology of personal achievement to a group of high-school juniors and seniors. It included a section on self-discipline. I used saving money as an example of something that required self-discipline. After class, one of the junior girls asked if she could talk to me at lunch. A few hours later she told me she had a great part-time job, and was taking home more than a hundred dollars a week. Then she said, "But I blow it all." She wanted me to be more specific about self-discipline and saving. I asked her what she spent her money on. She said, "Things . . . and fun." I asked her if she could get by with a few less things and a little less fun. She said yes, and we set up a plan in which she put forty dollars every week into a savings account before she spent any of her paycheck.

What she gave up: a few movies and rock concerts, a few cassettes and CDs, designer labels, fast food, and junk.

What she got: A few days before she graduated, she showed me her savings passbook. The bottom line read $4,851.20, a lot of money for a high-school kid in 1990. She had often put in more than forty dollars, and she'd earned interest that was compounded. In addition to the savings, she got a practical lesson in economics, an invaluable experience in self-discipline, confidence in her ability to handle money, a great sense of accomplishment, and increased self-esteem. She said the experience also helped her understand that the best things in life don't cost anything.

3. Several years ago I was a kid with the dream of playing professional basketball in the NBA. I was tall, had some athletic ability, and a burning desire. From grammar school through college, I worked at developing my body and my skills, and played basketball every chance I got. But I never made it to the NBA. I just wasn't good enough. But all the hard work wasn't in vain. There *was* a payoff—it was just different than the one I'd expected.

What I gave up: some of my leisure time, winter ski trips, parties during the season, and loafing.

What I got: the joy of sports, awards and recognition, a full scholarship to an outstanding university (worth about $150,000 today), great teammates, a college education and a degree, travel throughout the United States (including Hawaii), good work habits, valuable training in self-discipline, and a passion for staying in good physical condition.

In each of these three cases, compare the things that were given up with what was gained by doing it. Then answer these questions:

- Which choice had the longer-lasting results?
- Which choice developed character?
- Which choice was more meaningful?

Now answer these two:
- What's something you really want?
- What are you willing to give up to get it?

SELF-DISCIPLINE MEANS GOOD HABITS

Success is the sum of small efforts, repeated day in and day out. . . .

ROBERT COLLIER

The three cases mentioned previously involved making choices. They also involved forming habits. That's essentially what self-discipline is: making the right choices and forming good habits. We accomplish big things by doing small things over and over. In other words: practice, practice, practice is still the best path to achievement, no matter what it is. As we develop good habits, we experience a buildup of results. We also experience increased feelings of fulfillment. They're the natural outcome of accomplishment. The process might be summarized in this simple formula:

Right choices → Good habits → Accomplishment → Fulfillment

Most people either watch things happen or wonder later what happened. Self-discipline helps us *make* things happen. Good habits help us get things done when they need to be done, not when we feel like doing them. This is the key to being productive. It's also one of the keys to happiness. Self-discipline is the way we turn our capabilities into skills and our potential into reality. Rarely do we feel happier than when we reap the rewards of our consistent hard work.

True discipline isn't on your back needling you with imperatives; it is at your side, nudging you with incentives. When you understand that discipline is self-caring, not self-castigating, you won't cringe at its mention, but will cultivate it.

SYBIL STANTON

CHAPTER 15

Successful People Don't Find Time— They Make Time

Time is life. It is irreversible and irreplaceable. To waste your time is to waste your life, but to master your time is to master your life and make the most of it.

ALAN LAKEIN

ONE OF THE ESSENTIAL SKILLS OF LIFE

You're making absolutely fabulous use of your time right now—you're reading my book. If you use the rest of your time as wisely, you probably don't need to read this chapter. But if you occasionally feel as though your time and your life are marching in opposite directions, you might find a few helpful suggestions here. The previous four chapters have focused on skills that can help you turn your potential into reality: motivation, goal-setting, hard work, and self-discipline. There's one more: effective use of time. If you can combine it with the other four, you'll be among that small percentage of people who've learned to manage their time and their lives successfully.

More than two hundred years ago, Benjamin Franklin wrote that time is opportunity, and that in order to live fully, we have to learn to make the most of it. If we love life, he said, we'll treasure our time. We'll use it wisely. His famous autobiography is full of examples of how he mastered it.

Even though they don't teach time management in our schools, we now have more resources for learning about it than ever before. There are more than a hundred books on the subject, in addition to a wide variety of calendars and planners, as well as several software programs. I particularly like the management materials produced by Stephen Covey because he always places emphasis on spending *quality* time rather than simply finding out how to use time to be more productive. Covey introduced this concept in his classic book *The 7 Habits of Highly Effective People* and explained it more fully in his next book, *First Things First*. In the latter, Covey says, ". . . we get busier and busier doing 'good' things and never even stop to ask ourselves if what we're doing really matters most."

The most important step is to develop a new way of looking at time. We need to view it as a resource. It's always there, but like any other resource, it can be put to good use or it can be wasted. But there's one big difference between this resource and others: we can't save it, store it up, stockpile it, or hoard it. We can't turn it on or off, and we can't replace it. We're forced to spend it minute by minute. And once we spend it, we can't retrieve it. That's why the way we spend our time is the way we measure the quality of our lives. Time *is* life.

WINNERS AND LOSERS: WHAT THEY DO WITH TIME

Always concentrate on the most valuable use of your time. This is what separates the winners from the losers.

BRIAN TRACY

One of the main themes of this book is expressed in the title of Chapter 4: "We Live by Choice, Not by Chance." Nowhere is this more evident than in the choices we make about how to use our time. This is what separates the winners in life from the losers. It isn't luck, genetics, timing, or knowing the right people. It's what we do with the 168 hours that we get each week. There are some distinct differences between the way winners and losers view time, talk about time, and use time. Here are some examples:

Losers:	*Winners:*
They kill time.	They use time.
They waste time.	They spend time wisely.
They lose time.	They value time.
They let time slip away.	They organize their time.
They take time for granted.	They treasure time.
They squander time.	They schedule time.
They can't find time.	They make time.

I don't want to imply here that anyone who's ever wasted time is a loser. We all do that occasionally. I'm talking about people who waste so much of their time that they end up wasting their lives. I also don't want to imply that having fun or relaxing is a waste of time. I emphasized the importance of that in Chapter 3. Some people actually need to schedule more of it into their lives. The key is balance. The main point here is that the people who succeed in life understand that time is their most valuable resource. It's a resource that's distributed evenly. Everyone gets twenty-four hours a day. It's what we do with it that defines our lives.

WE HAVE ALL THE TIME WE NEED

We have more timesaving devices than ever before, and each year several new high-tech products come out that are guaranteed to save us even more time. Yet, never have people complained so much about not having enough time. Not long ago, the results of a Gallup Poll appeared in the *San Francisco Chronicle*. The headline read: "People Feel Time Is Running Out." As the article continues on the next page, the headline reads, "Americans Feel Pressed for Time." It opens with these words: "The American fight against the clock is a pervasive phenomenon. . . ." The authors explain that almost eighty percent of the people in this country feel that time moves too fast for them and that they can't do all the things they want to do. Something is obviously wrong.

What's wrong is people's thinking about time. They're making two basic errors. To begin with, time isn't moving any faster now that it did when the first clock was made. There are still sixty minutes in each hour. Second, there's a simple reason why people can't do all the things they want to do: they want to do too much. Maybe they believe that commercial that says, "You can have it all." But the truth is, you can't. And as I said in the last chapter, you have to give up something to get something. Anyone who thinks he's going to have it all and do it all is never going to have enough time.

About two months after the Gallup Poll was published, another article appeared in the *Chronicle* about people who'd re-examined their priorities. They'd looked especially closely at the ways they were spending time and didn't like what they saw. What they did was cut back: on their drive for status and power and on their need to "have it all." They simplified their lives and said they had more time for relaxing and doing enjoyable things. Actually, they didn't have any more time than they had before. They just chose to spend it differently.

They learned to treasure it. They learned to make time for the things that are truly important. It's no surprise that they also said the quality of their lives had improved.

I hear people of all ages say that they don't have enough time. But that's simply not the truth. What they really mean is that they don't know how to manage the time they have. Most people don't discover, as Stephen Covey did, that effective use of time is a skill. Using time effectively, like operating a computer, is a skill that can be acquired. The better we become at the skill, the more efficient we become. Then we begin to realize that there really is plenty of time. The old expression that says we can always make time for things that are important is just as true today as it was the first time it was said.

Time hasn't changed. We have. Experts throughout the ages have been telling us that there's plenty of time. Here are a few of them:

There is a time for everything, and a season for every activity under heaven. . . .

ECCLESIASTES 3:1
KING SOLOMON, 925 B.C.

We always have time enough, if we will but use it right.
GOETHE, GERMAN PHILOSOPHER, 1700s

We never shall have more time. We have, and we have always had, all the time there is.

ARNOLD BENNETT, ENGLISH WRITER, 1910

There is no such thing as lack of time. We all have plenty of time to do everything we really want to do.

ALAN LAKEIN, TIME-EFFICIENCY EXPERT, 1973

Every morning when the alarm goes off, we have a totally new opportunity to do what we want with the hours we have been gifted. And we are gifted with that clean slate every day for the rest of our lives.

HYRUM SMITH,
ORIGINATOR OF THE FRANKLIN PLANNER, 2000

FOUR KEYS TO MASTERING YOUR TIME AND YOUR LIFE

There are several books and seminar programs devoted entirely to personal-time management, so it would be presumptuous of me to think that I can teach you in just a few pages how to become an expert. But when we develop any skill, we always start with the basics. There are four which I find invaluable. They're easy to understand but more difficult to apply if it involves changing habits. But that's what effective time management is: good choices and good habits.

1. Plan your day

A successful life is nothing more than a string of successful days. So why not make the most of each one? Contractors have building plans, executives have business plans, coaches have game plans, and teachers have lesson plans. The reason is obvious, so why not a day plan? It doesn't have to be anything elaborate, and it doesn't take much time, but it works.

Some people call it making a "to do" list; I call it daily goal-setting. Whatever you call it, virtually every successful person does it in some form.

Of all the positive ways to invest your time, this is number one. If you'll set aside ten minutes each day (the night before or first thing in the morning), write down the things you want to accomplish, number them in order of importance, and keep your list visible throughout the day, you'll be amazed at how much more effective and productive you become.

Check off each daily goal as you complete it. This is the rewarding part. Sense of accomplishment is one of the best feelings we can have. It feels great to get something done and then be able to record it. It also shows progress. If you're getting things done daily, you're living productively. This is an important part of the process. Daily accomplishments are the building blocks of a successful life.

2. Make appointments with yourself

Let's say you have a task that will require about two hours of work and needs to be done by next Thursday. Most people say to themselves, "I've got to get that done by next week." Notice the difference when you say instead, "I'm going to do it Tuesday between four and six P.M." Remember, the mind only moves toward specifics. If you say to a friend, "Let's get together someday," it'll never happen. But if you make an appointment with your friend, it *will* happen. We tend to keep our appointments.

If you have something that needs to be done, but you're likely to put it off until the last minute, there's a simple solution: Make an appointment with yourself. Before you do anything else, make the decision that it's going to get done. Then decide *when* you're going to do it, and commit yourself to that specific time. As simple as it sounds, this technique not only helps you get more done but also has some side benefits: it develops self-discipline, aids in goal-setting, helps overcome procrastination, and teaches you to use your time more effectively.

3. Use the little-bit-at-a-time approach

One of the most effective ways of getting major tasks completed is by doing them a little at a time. Instead of waiting for the right mood or the right amount of time to come along, block out specific periods in your daily schedule. This works best when the period set aside is at the same time each day. The key is being consistent. That's when it becomes a habit.

You get used to doing it, and each day part of the task gets accomplished. Let's use writing a book as an example. It seems like an overwhelming job when looked on as a whole. But if you write only one page a day, even if you take Saturdays and Sundays off, you'll have a 260-page book written by the end of the year.

This technique could also be compared to building a brick house. The individual bricks are pretty small, and the process of laying them only one at a time looks painfully slow. But those bricks, when one is constantly added to another, become something much greater than small blocks of building material. We can use small blocks of time in much the same way. Success is the result of hard work done little by little, day by day.

4. Know your most productive time

All people seem to have "body clocks." There's a certain time during the day when one person feels the most productive, yet someone else might be completely ineffective at that same time. Some of us are morning people; others are night people. Some people fade in the middle of the afternoon, while others are just getting charged up. No two people seem to be the same. The important thing is to recognize your own clock—when you're likely to function best. This should be

1970s, some Bay Area psychologists began teaching people how to become self-actualized and started the human-potential movement. In the 1980s, a powerful member of the California Assembly said that the root of all society's problems was people feeling poorly about themselves, and the self-esteem movement, begun earlier, was officially sanctioned.

It was joined first by educators, then by parents and people who work in the social services. Eventually, even the business community bought into it. Self-esteem experts seemed to be coming from everywhere. They all had a program and a new way for us to feel better about ourselves. And much of the movement became downright silly. Among other things, I've read and been told that I can improve my self-esteem by blowing myself a kiss in the mirror each time I walk by it, by repeating the mantra "I am special" over and over, by wearing a button that says "I am lovable and capable," by getting twelve hugs a day, by being "validated" or "empowered" by other people, by changing my hairstyle, by writing all my problems on a piece of paper and then throwing it in the wastebasket, or by plopping down up to two thousand dollars for an intense weekend of rebuilding my inner self. Nonsense.

Some of the silliness continued through the 1990s, but the self-esteem movement was starting to lose a bit of its luster. We were more into making money. That's what was making a lot of people feel good about themselves—they had more things. "He who dies with the most toys wins" was a popular bumper sticker of the decade. Many people were starting to confuse self-esteem with downright selfishness.

part of your daily planning. Schedule yourself, if possible, to do your most important work during these hours. This is what's meant by maximizing time.

A FINAL WORD

How can I write an entire chapter about using time effectively, and barely mention procrastination? Isn't that the biggest problem regarding time? Most people say it is, but I'm not convinced that procrastinating is always bad. Everyone does it to some extent. There are some people who actually function better by putting things off until the last moment, and then coming through under pressure. But they're an exception. Most people feel both inefficient and guilty when they procrastinate.

I haven't focused on it in here because if you follow the suggestions for using time effectively, you won't be concerned about procrastination. You won't have time to feel guilty about putting things off because you'll be too busy getting things done. When you realize that your time is your life, you figure out ways to make the most of it. Success depends on effective use of time. Successful people don't find time; they make time.

Make the best use of your time, despite all the difficulties of these days.

EPHESIANS 5:16

CHAPTER 16

No One Else Can Raise Your Self-esteem

Self-esteem is that deep-down inside the skin feeling you have of your own self-worth.

DENIS WAITLEY

ANOTHER CALIFORNIA TREND

In his famous book *Megatrends,* John Naisbitt calls California the bellwether state of trendsetting. It's a place where new ways of thinking and doing things often begin. In the 1960s, California's flower children began questioning our traditional values and started the peace-and-love movement. In the

Maybe because so many marketers and advertisers were telling us to be good to ourselves because we deserved it.

Do I sound like I'm against self-esteem? I'm not. In fact, I'm one hundred percent in favor of it. What I'm not in favor of is the movement as it took shape. It began with good intentions, but got off the track—*way* off the track. Too many people who didn't understand what self-esteem is or where it comes from, and too many others who were out to make big bucks from that confusion, not only distorted the movement but turned it into an object of ridicule. And too many young people were being told that everything they did was good, whether it was or not. That was not only wrong but damaging. Teachers across the country were playing "feel-good" games with their classes in the hope of enhancing self-esteem. What they were really doing was setting their students up with false expectations of how things work in the real world.

FALSE VS. REAL SELF-ESTEEM

While I was attending a state conference on self-esteem, one of the keynote speakers was Bill Honig, then the highly respected California Superintendent of Public Instruction. He didn't give the standard, inspirational, "You-can-make-all-your-students-feel-good-about-themselves" speech. Instead, he shared honestly with the thousands of teachers in attendance what his concerns were about self-esteem and its place in our schools. He said he was all in favor of helping our students raise their self-esteem, but his major concern was what he called "false self-esteem." He said, "You can tell a kid all day long that he's wonderful, whether he is or not, and it might make him feel good. But then he goes out into the real world expecting the same thing, and he gets crushed." Mr. Honig emphasized that the best way to enhance a student's self-esteem is to give him the tools that he can use to better his life.

Finally, someone was getting to the truth of the matter. I wanted to run up and give him a big hug when he was finished. But I restrained myself, and gave him a simple handshake instead. I did have the opportunity to talk briefly with him. I said I shared his concern about false self-esteem, and was glad that someone of his stature had addressed it. He said, "I wish more of these well-meaning teachers understood that self-esteem will take care of itself if we can help our students learn the skills and attitudes they need to be successful."

What, then, is *real* self-esteem? Of all the definitions I've seen, I think the best is the one by Denis Waitley that I used at the beginning of this chapter. I like his phrase "deep-down inside the skin." That's where real self-esteem is felt. It isn't something another person can give to us. It's how we truly feel about ourselves, even when no one else is around. If self-esteem is real, it comes from within. By itself, the word *esteem* means "to appreciate the worth of, to hold in high regard, to have genuine respect." So self-esteem is really self-respect.

It's how we genuinely feel about ourselves, regardless of what others say. And how we feel about ourselves is closely related to how our character develops. That's why the

California Task Force on Self-Esteem, a group of dedicated people who met regularly and conducted research for two years, emphasized personal and social responsibility in its final report. We can only feel good about ourselves when our behavior is positive and we can be fully accountable for it. Ultimately, the development of personal character is both a choice and a responsibility. Other people may help or hinder, but we build our own character, and with it, we determine our level of self-esteem. It's strictly an inside job.

FROM DEPENDENCE TO INDEPENDENCE

There *is* a time in our lives when both our self-image and our self-esteem are determined by other people. When we're small children, our lives are dominated by adults and older kids. We see ourselves through the messages we receive from them. Good messages, good self-image. Bad messages, bad self-image. The point is that when we're at a tender age, we respond to the messages we hear most often. We form a picture of ourselves, and then we develop feelings that are consistent with it. We tend to become what we're told about ourselves.

But one of the most important things to understand about self-esteem is that as we get older we have to learn to think for ourselves (Chapter 5). We need to realize that we have a choice (Chapter 4) about how we're going to respond to the messages from other people. Eleanor Roosevelt once said, "No one can make you feel inferior without your consent." It would follow, then, that no one can make you feel *anything* without your consent.

It's what we believe about ourselves that counts. Whether we were treated rightly or wrongly as children, our self-esteem is now our responsibility.

Don't get me wrong. I'm not saying that other people aren't important in regard to our feelings. All of us need to be told from time to time that we're loved, appreciated, and valued. We need our hugs, too. It's not only necessary, but fantastic, to be affirmed by other people. That's why I wrote Chapter 10. But we can't sit around and wait for others to applaud us in order to feel good. We have to do things that make us feel good about ourselves even without the praise. Then when it comes, it reaffirms what we're already feeling. It's a great bonus.

Other people can do a lot of things to make us feel good. But, ultimately, how we feel about ourselves is the direct result of what *we* do and what *we* think. Real self-esteem is respect that we have to earn from ourselves.

THE INGREDIENTS OF SELF-ESTEEM

I can remember having feelings of low self-esteem for many years, even though I was working hard and finding a lot of success in my career and in a few other areas of my life. But I still didn't like or respect myself, and I didn't know why. I found out that hard work and a successful career aren't enough. I was missing the key ingredients. I couldn't be comfortable with myself because I didn't have the right combination. It's like opening one of those combination locks. It doesn't work unless you have *all* the numbers.

Eventually, I discovered the missing parts, and my self-esteem rose dramatically. It was nice to both like and respect myself. I guess I'm a slow learner, because it sure took a long time. But better late than never. Some people never do figure out the combination. That brings me back to some of the reasons I wrote this book: (1) I want to help other people discover that combination, hopefully earlier than I did; (2) I think our me-centered society has bombarded us with the wrong messages; (3) I think we need to know the difference between self-worship and self-esteem; and (4) I believe we have incredible potential for genuine success and self-respect.

Actually, the ingredients of self-esteem are quite simple. The problem is that so many people with different ideas and motives jumped on the bandwagon; they made it look far more complicated than it really is. That's because so many of them had a new program to sell. In the first place, self-esteem isn't something we can buy. We can't pursue it, look for it, or find it. And as I said earlier, we can't get it from other people. Real self-esteem is a by-product. Feeling good about ourselves is the natural result of doing the right things and thinking the right thoughts. Despite what the self-styled gurus and experts tell us, self-esteem is part of a natural process.

If you can be consistent in the following four areas of life, you'll never have to worry about healthy self-esteem. It'll be your constant companion.

1. *Be kind*—It's impossible to feel good about ourselves when we're mean, selfish, or insensitive. How we deal with other people has a mirror effect. It always reflects back on us. The better we treat others, the better we feel about ourselves. The more we build and affirm people, the more we grow as human beings. Remember, good people build their lives on a foundation of respect (Chapter 8).

2. *Be honorable*—I have yet to read about any connection between honesty and self-esteem. But I'm convinced that it's an absolute essential. You could take every self-esteem course in existence, but if you're dishonest you have no right to feel good about yourself. And I guarantee that you won't. Integrity is the cornerstone of high self-esteem. As long as you have it, you'll always be respected, by others and by yourself. Remember, honesty is still the best policy (Chapter 9).

3. *Be productive*—One of the "seven deadly sins" of the Middle Ages was sloth, which means idleness or laziness. My sons used to call people who sat around and did nothing "slugs." I thought it was a great term. It's pretty hard to feel good about yourself when you're being a slug. Being productive—learning, planning, achieving—is what builds self-esteem. Remember, there's no substitute for hard work (Chapter 13).

4. *Be positive*—We can't feel good about ourselves if our heads are full of negative thoughts. If we're treating others with respect, being honest, and achieving something with our lives,

then we need to give ourselves credit. It's healthy to develop a good attitude about ourselves. Remember, attitude is a choice—the most important one you'll ever make (Chapter 5).

Self-esteem is the reputation you have with yourself.
BRIAN TRACY

CHAPTER 17

The Body Needs Nutrition and Exercise— So Do the Mind and Spirit

. . . Mind, body, and spirit act in concert to determine health and well-being.

DR. CARL THORESEN

LIFE IS A BALANCING ACT

Thousands of years ago the ancient Chinese, and later the great Greek philosophers, examined life from three perspectives: physical, mental, and spiritual. While they didn't interpret them in exactly the same way, they did agree on their existence and that each one was as important as the other. They also agreed that as we learn to balance these parts of our nature, we grow in understanding, become more complete as human beings, and live more fully. The problem today is that too many people, regardless of age, try to live one- or two-dimensional lives in a three-dimensional world.

That's because on the way to the twenty-first century and all its technological wonders, those three dimensions of life somehow became a blur. The high-tech world we now live in makes it possible to go places, acquire things, and receive information at an almost dizzying speed. While that's fantastic and exciting, there *is* a downside. The more we get caught up in the incredibly fast pace and conveniences of modern life, the less we take time to think. It's easier to let our electronic devices do it for us. And eventually, we end up wondering how to make sense out of life.

Fortunately, knowledge from history and ancient philosophy is still with us, and modern-day thinkers are now suggesting that we need to pay more attention to some of the great lessons of the past. The age-old teaching that we need to balance the physical, mental, and spiritual dimensions of our lives is taking on more meaning than ever. We're discovering that no matter how great our technology is, it can't produce either happiness or fulfillment.

CARING FOR THE BODY

Our body is a machine for living. It is organized for that; it is its nature. Let life go on in it.

LEO TOLSTOY

I was in a store a few years ago when I noticed a man wearing a T-shirt that said, "If I'd known I was going to live this long, I would have taken better care of myself." I got a good chuckle out of it. Then I checked him out a little more closely. I realized he was about my age. He was also overweight and looked kind of worn out, maybe hung over. I thought, "Well, at least he can laugh at himself." But I suspect there was a ring of truth in his message. He probably *did* wish that he'd taken better care of himself.

At no time in our history have we been more aware of the benefits of caring for the body. We have knowledge about nutrition and exercise that wasn't available as recently as ten years ago. And we've experienced a genuine fitness explosion. People of all ages are paying closer attention to what goes into their bodies and are becoming more physically active. And they're living longer, healthier, and more productive lives.

The physical-fitness crusade is one of the few bandwagons that I recommend jumping onto, but for the duration, not just the short ride. It's been well publicized, and there's plenty of good information available, so I see no need to repeat it here. Nor do I see a need to warn you about the evils of tobacco, drugs, and alcohol. I have a lot of confidence in people who read books like this. They want to succeed in life and are smart enough to know that it won't happen if they poison their own bodies.

There are just two points I want to make about physical fitness. The first is that it helps to have a practical attitude about the role of your body. It's not the most essential thing about you, but it's the vehicle that carries what *is* essential. If you were told when you got your first car that it would be your only one, that it would have to last a lifetime, I suspect that you'd take excellent care of it. That's the way it is with your body—it's the only one you'll ever have. It'll run better and last longer if you take care of it.

Second, while keeping the body in good condition is important, how it looks in comparison to other bodies is *not* important. You don't have to qualify for the cover of *Muscle* magazine or the swimsuit issue of *Sports Illustrated* in order to be in shape and feel good about yourself. Part of my workout routine includes weight training, but I'll never look like Arnold Schwarzenegger. That's because there are as many different body types as there are faces. Being concerned about how other bodies look and function doesn't improve the quality of our lives. Taking good care of our own body does.

CARING FOR THE MIND

The mind is a bit like a garden. If it isn't fed and cultivated, weeds will take it over.

ERWIN G. HALL

I doubt that anyone would disagree that a body functions better when it gets the right combination of nutrition and exercise. How about the mind? It hasn't received the same kind of publicity that the body has in recent years, but it too needs nutrition and exercise in order to operate at maximum efficiency. If we don't pay attention to what's going into it and how we're using it, it starts to bog down.

MENTAL DIET

How well would your body function if all you ate was ice cream, candy bars, doughnuts, potato chips, and cookies, and if all you drank were soft drinks? Don't get me wrong—I'm not suggesting a ban on all those things. In fact, I've been known to indulge in a few of these "fun foods" myself. But a steady diet of them, without the nutrients the body needs, would do anyone in.

How well would your mind function if all you read was the *National Enquirer,* if all you watched on TV were soap operas, big-time wrestling, and Jerry Springer, if the only thing you listened to were rap and heavy-metal music, and if the only movies you saw were *Scary Movie* and *Dumb and Dumber*? I'm not condemning any of them, but what if those were the only things going into your head? Your mind would turn to mush. The brain needs nutrients, too.

MENTAL EXERCISE

How well would your body function if you were a totally committed couch potato—if your main activity of the day was getting in and out of bed and if your goal in life was to become a full-fledged "slug"? Muscles that aren't used atrophy—they waste away.

How well would your mind function if you left it in neutral most of the time, if you thought *learning* was a dirty word, and "vegging" was your idea of mental stimulation? The mind that isn't used will also atrophy.

Obviously, the examples I've given here are pretty extreme. I used them with both my high-school and university students for years, and they were always good for a laugh. But they also helped make a point. After one class activity, one of my adult students said to me, "I'm glad we did this. We need to pay more attention to the garbage that's being dumped into our heads every day. It happens without us even being aware of it." That *was* the point.

The advertising industry blitzes us relentlessly; the news media tells us everything that's wrong in the world; the entertainment business gives us an abundance of trash; and we're around people who do a lot of complaining. That's not exactly a healthy mental diet. But remember, we live by choice. We need to be just as selective about what goes into our minds as we are about what goes into our bodies. We can't control all the garbage, but we *can* be more aware of it and learn to screen much of it out.

We can also get into the habit of making sure that healthy things are going into our minds. An older and wiser friend of mine told me several years ago that he begins every day on a positive note. He sets aside time each morning to read something that's uplifting and thought-provoking. He said it not only helps him focus on what's good about life but also helps him screen out a lot of the negative. Shortly afterward, I started doing the same. Guess what. It works! It's probably my best habit.

We make two important choices regarding our minds:

1. What we let into them
2. How we use them

We can let the right things in by being selective about what we read, hear, and watch, and who we associate with. We can use our minds to think, solve problems, learn, and be creative. Someone once said that the mind is a terrible thing to waste. Why would anyone want to waste such a marvelous instrument? When it's nourished and used constructively, it can help us both to appreciate life and to live it more fully.

CARING FOR THE SPIRIT

On the bookshelf of life, God is a useful work of reference, always at hand but seldom consulted.

DAG HAMMARSKJÖLD

These first two dimensions of life—physical and mental—are easy to understand. They're more obvious because we're aware that we use our bodies and minds every day. Understanding our spiritual nature isn't so simple. In the first place, it's less obvious. We're often *not* aware of it. Secondly, the word *spiritual* means different things to different people.

Because of that, you should know where I'm coming from. Resolving the spiritual issues of life was one of my greatest struggles, so I've been all over the landscape. At various stages I've been an agnostic, a Catholic, an atheist, a humanist, a Protestant, and a blend of some of the great Eastern religions. I've studied Judaism, Islam, and Hinduism, and spent a year devoted to meditation. And during other times, I simply believed the same thing as the last attractive woman I'd met. But that didn't work either, and I kept coming up empty. So I continued to search.

Where did all of this bring me? It brought me to the teachings of Jesus Christ. I became a Christian when I was thirty-nine. It was a profoundly life-changing decision. To this day, I'm still amazed at how the parts of a fragmented life finally came together. While I'll never be able to fully explain it, I believe in a God who was powerful enough to create the universe, yet is personal enough to want an intimate relationship with each of us. I pray every day. I belong to a great church and attend it regularly. I study the Bible and try to apply its principles to my life. I believe in a place called heaven and hope to be there someday.

But you also need to know that I don't think I'm a saint, I'm not holy, and I don't have all the answers. I don't always succeed in applying those biblical principles, and I don't go around asking people if they've been "saved" or "born again." I'm a long way from being perfect, but I'm making progress. And I don't mind admitting that I need God's help to stay on the right track.

I realize that many of my readers don't have the same beliefs. That's not a problem. I taught a course called World Religions at the University of San Francisco for several years. That experience and my own search for inner peace helped me develop a great respect for what other people believe and don't believe. And a basic tenet of my own faith is not to judge others. Besides, I didn't write this just for people who share my faith. I wrote it for people who want to make the most of their lives. I'm not saying that you have to believe what I do in order to be happy. What I *am* saying is that you might greatly enrich your life by exploring and developing your spiritual nature.

When Mikhail Gorbachev granted religious freedom to the people in the former Soviet Union in the early nineties, he said he did it because of what he saw in other countries. He said that people who practice their faith and live by their principles seem to enjoy life at a deeper level. It took the Russians seventy-five years to figure that out. It took me thirty-nine. I hope it takes you less.

WHY OUR SPIRITUAL NATURE IS OFTEN IGNORED

These are the most common reasons why people avoid having anything to do with spirituality or religion:

- No experiences with it or knowledge of it
- Bad previous experiences (especially being dragged to church as a kid)

- Things are going good; can't see a need for it
- Don't believe in God
- Believe in God, but not in organized religion
- Don't like the way some churchgoing people behave; they're hypocrites
- The TV preachers are a turn-off; they're also crooks
- Church is boring
- God (religion) is an escape from reality

I've not only heard all these excuses, I've *used* most of them. It's not my purpose to refute all of them here, but I do want to address the last one.

BECOMING COMPLETE

The more complete and integrated we become, the better we feel about ourselves and life in general. An important step in that direction is ridding ourselves of the notion that anything pertaining to God involves an escape from reality or an attempt to take the easy way out. I think it's just the opposite. Exploring our spiritual nature is a move *toward* becoming complete, not away from it. And there's nothing easy about it. It's much more difficult to explore the depths of our souls than it is to dismiss our entire spiritual nature. What's easy is to ignore God and to reject all religion with simpleminded explanations of why it doesn't work. In *The Road Less Traveled*, Scott Peck says that ". . . the journey of spiritual growth requires courage and initiative and independence of thought and action." He adds that it's often lonely and difficult because we live in a society that wants quick and easy answers, even to life's most complex questions. But life is difficult, and that includes the spiritual part.

A book that had a profound effect on my thinking about the spiritual part of life was *No Man Is an Island,* by Thomas Merton. I read it at a time when I was feeling both fragmented and empty, and it helped me understand why. Merton says we too often focus our lives on the immediate satisfaction of material things. We ignore our spiritual nature because it isn't something we can see or touch, so we think it isn't real. Merton believes the opposite. He considers the spiritual life to be part of our search for the real self. It's what sustains us and gives us hope when those material things lose their meaning. Merton helped me realize that I needed to put my spiritual life in order before I could feel integrated and complete.

Dag Hammarskjöld, the Nobel Peace Prize winner who was head of the United Nations from 1953 to 1961, wrote in *Markings* that the search for God is not an escape but a fulfillment—the only way to have a real understanding of life. He felt that a relationship with God was necessary for overcoming our narrow self-interest and for developing the knowledge that helps us become complete human beings. When we begin to live in that relationship with God, we also begin to live for others. We do this, he says, in order to save both our soul and our self-esteem.

I realize this is pretty heavy stuff, especially if you've never given much thought to your spiritual life. It would have been easier and safer to leave this topic out. But it's too important, and I wouldn't be true to myself if I didn't include it. I want to urge my readers, as I urged my students, to develop themselves to the fullest. And I don't think that can happen when the spiritual part of life is ignored. It doesn't have to be, because some of the most valuable and practical wisdom the world has ever known still lies recorded in the great holy books of history. For thousands of years they've helped people understand that there's a relationship between spiritual development, character, and overall well-being.

As the body and mind need to be nourished and exercised, so does the spirit. It can be nourished by seeking answers to life's toughest questions: Where did I come from? Why am I here? Where am I going? In looking for the answers, we not only feed and develop our spiritual nature, we make important discoveries about life and ourselves. One of those discoveries is that the time-honored values of honesty and kindness lie at the heart of all great spiritual teachings. There's no better way to exercise the spirit.

Those who have grown the most spiritually are those who are experts in living. And there is yet another joy, even greater. It is the joy of communion with God.

M. SCOTT PECK

CHAPTER 18

It's OK to Fail—
Everyone Else Has

If you're willing to accept failure and learn from it, if you're willing to consider failure as a blessing in disguise and bounce back, you've got the potential of harnessing one of the most powerful success forces.

JOSEPH SUGARMAN

EVERYONE FAILS

Finally, I get to write about a subject on which I'm an expert: failure. I'm not alone, though, because everyone fails. Not some, not most, but everyone. Ask the most successful people you know if they've ever failed at anything, and you'll get two responses. The first will be either a reflective smile or a laugh. The second will be a question something like this: "Which one of my failures would you like to hear about?" Failing is a fact of life, a necessary part of the process that no one escapes. It isn't *whether* we fail that matters; it's *how* we fail. The difference between the people who succeed in life and the ones who don't isn't found in the number of times they fail. It's found in what they do *after* they fail.

Two Famous Failures

I started reading biographies when I was twelve. After becoming a history major in college, that practice increased significantly. I continue to read biographies today because I discovered that they're the best books ever written on the subject of success. But they're not just about success; they're also about failure. That's because all people who've become famous for their accomplishments have also tasted bitter defeat and disappointment. None of them succeeded without failing first. The key was how they used their failures.

Two of the most famous failures I can think of are Albert Einstein and Thomas Edison. Our greatest mathematician and our greatest inventor, long before they were honored for their achievements, suffered through years of trial and error, mistakes, disappointment, frustration, and defeat. Neither would have become the success he did had he not been willing to learn from his setbacks and keep trying in times of adversity. The failures of these two great men aren't as well known as their accomplishments, but they're just as important.

When Edison was looking for ways to keep a lightbulb

burning, he tried more than ten thousand different combinations of materials that flopped. When someone asked him how he could continue after failing that many times, he said he didn't see it as failure. He said that he'd successfully identified over ten thousand ways that didn't work and that each attempt brought him closer to the one that would. Einstein, reputed to be the smartest person who ever lived, said, "I think and think for months and years. Ninety-nine times the conclusion is false. The hundredth time I am right."

Failing is a natural outcome of trying. Success rarely comes on the first attempt. If we think it does, all we're doing is setting ourselves up for a big fall, one that might keep us from getting up and trying again. Success comes only as the result of time, determination, and prolonged effort. Edison and Einstein were perfect examples. Both were called geniuses, but neither liked that title. Remember, it was Edison himself who gave us that famous definition of genius: "one percent inspiration and ninety-nine percent perspiration." The problem with too many people today is that they're not willing to perspire long enough, if at all. They want their success instantly. But it rarely comes that way. We have to be willing to fail first.

What We Can Learn from Failure

I divide the world into learners and nonlearners. There are people who learn, who are open to what happens around them, who listen, who hear the lessons. When

*they do something stupid, they don't do it again. And
when they do something that works a little bit, they do
it even better and harder the next time. The question to
ask is not whether you are a success or a failure, but
whether you are a learner or a nonlearner.*

BENJAMIN BARBER

Failure is one of life's greatest teachers. That is, it *can* be if
we choose to learn from it rather than be crushed by it. These
are some of its best lessons:

- Failure teaches us humility. It confronts us with our
  limitations and shows us that we're not invincible.

- Failure teaches us to correct our course of action. It
  forces us to look at what we're doing and gives us the
  opportunity to try a new direction.

- Failure teaches us that we can't always have what we
  want. Sometimes, even when we do all the right things,
  it still doesn't work out.

- Failure teaches us about the strength of our character. It
  challenges us to dig deeper into our resources when we
  experience setbacks.

- Failure teaches us about perseverance. It asks us

whether we're going to quit or become more determined and keep trying.

• Failure teaches us that we can survive defeat. There's no shame in falling, only in being afraid to get up and try again.

There's one more thing that we can learn from failure, and it's the most valuable lesson of all. Failure can make us stronger. That's the theme of a wonderful book I discovered when I was working on the first draft of this book. It's called *When Smart People Fail,* by Carole Hyatt and Linda Gottlieb. The authors, having experienced and overcome shattering setbacks themselves, wanted to know how others had dealt with failure. They interviewed almost two hundred people, many of them famous, who had also suffered major defeats. While reading about people's failings doesn't exactly sound like a positive experience, it was exactly that. Rather than a book of gloom, it's a book of hope, and I found it tremendously inspiring. It made me realize that I hadn't stopped pounding on myself for mistakes of the past, and it helped me focus instead on what I'd learned from them.

One of the main points in the book is that most people don't realize that hidden in our failures are sources of growth and renewed strength. Too often we don't see the benefits that can come after we fall flat on our faces. We need to learn, especially when we're young, that failure is nothing to be ashamed of. Real strength comes from discovering that we can not only survive but grow. One of the persons Hyatt and Gottlieb interviewed was Dr. Keith Reemstma. He's a surgeon who's been trying for years to find a cure for diabetes. But he still hasn't found it. What keeps him going? "I never think of what I do as failure," he says. "It's just an incomplete result. I always have in mind what I am trying to accomplish, and each experiment tells me a little more about what I have done wrong." What a great attitude! He sounds like Edison. Learning that we can overcome defeat makes us stronger, wiser, and tougher. It also gives us hope.

FAILURE GIVES US CHOICES

The question isn't *whether* we're going to fail, because all of us are. The question is *how* we're going to fail. We have two choices:

1. The wrong way to fail

There are two common mistakes we make regarding failure. The first one is trying too hard to avoid it. If we're afraid to fail, we play it so safe that we never take any risks. But risk is both an important part of success and a necessary condition of growth. Marva Collins, an extraordinary teacher from Chicago who helped thousands of kids rise above their dreadful conditions, had a favorite saying: "If you can't make a mistake, you can't make anything." If we're not willing to risk failure, we're not deserving of success. Success doesn't come *to* us; we have to go out and get it. That involves sticking our necks out a bit. Not risking failure is the worst failure of all.

The second mistake we make is to allow failure to defeat us. We get angry, frustrated, disappointed, discouraged. And too often, we give up and quit. I'm not saying these feelings aren't valid or real. There's nothing wrong with suffering after a big flop. But the suffering shouldn't destroy us. It should help us check our level of determination and our resolve to bounce back. Thousands of years ago Confucius said, "Our greatest glory is not in never falling, but in rising every time we fall."

2. The right way to fail

On the first page of this chapter, I said that our success is determined largely by what we do *after* we fail. Here are three suggestions for dealing with life's major fizzles: First, find someone whom you consider wise. Then just talk. You'll get your feelings out in a healthy way; you'll find out what your friend has learned from failure; you'll be reassured that you're not alone; and you'll get encouragement to bounce back. Second, go back to the drawing board. Literally, I mean sit down and start writing: about what you did, about how you feel, about your goal, and about what you're going to do next. You'll be amazed at what ends up on that paper. Third, read about some of the successful failures in our history. Reading the stories of people like Lincoln, Edison, Gandhi, Martin Luther King, Jr., and other famous failures can fill us with hope.

"Strong at the Broken Places"

Near the end of *A Farewell to Arms,* Ernest Hemingway's famous novel about World War I, he wrote, "The world breaks everyone and afterward many are strong at the broken places." The world does, indeed, break everyone, and usually not just once. But as a broken bone becomes even stronger when it heals, so do we. It all depends on our attitude and our choices. We can become stronger at our broken places if we choose to learn from our mistakes, correct our course, and try again. Our failures in life, as painful as they are, can be our most valuable learning experiences and our greatest source of renewed strength. As General George S. Patton said, "Success is how high you bounce after you hit bottom."

Don't be afraid to fail. Don't waste energy trying to cover up failure. Learn from your failures and go on to the next challenge. It's OK to fail. If you're not failing you're not growing.

H. Stanley Judd

CHAPTER 19

Life Is Simpler When We Know What's Essential

And now here is my secret, a very simple secret: It is only with the heart that one sees rightly; what is essential is invisible to the eye.

ANTOINE DE SAINT-EXUPÉRY, *THE LITTLE PRINCE*

A FEW SIMPLE RULES

Thousands of years ago a wise man named Confucius said life is actually quite simple and that it becomes complicated only because we insist on making it so. In more recent times a brilliant man named Einstein said we need to be reminded that even God always takes the simplest ways. While we live in a complex world, it doesn't mean we have to lead complicated lives. But we often do just that because we spend too much of our time struggling with life's complexities while ignoring its simplicities.

When I was a freshman in college, I met Hal DeJulio, someone who'd figured out how to both simplify and maximize his life. He was a successful alumnus who liked to return to the university and visit with the students. He's one of those rare individuals who does everything with a passion. He was full of energy and enthusiasm, he had an incredibly positive attitude, and he laughed a lot. He was a spirit-lifter: someone who's always upbeat and has something good to say. As we became friends, I became more and more curious about him. So one day I asked, "How'd you get this way? What makes you tick?" He said he started making good money in sales right out of college and found himself caught in the fast lane by the time he turned thirty. The more money he made, the more his life began to change. He discovered that making money wasn't everything and that he needed to do something to help keep his priorities straight.

So he took some time off and wrote a list of what was important to him. His original list had several things on it, but the more he examined it, the shorter it got. Finally, he'd reduced it to six. He took his wallet out and showed me a little card he kept inside. He said, "Once I got it down to six, I wrote them on this card under the heading 'SIMPLE RULES OF LIFE.' I promised myself that I'd look at it every day and live the rest of my life by these rules." Now in his late seventies, he's still guided by these rock-solid principles, and he still

has a passion for living. He never did show me his list, but he did encourage me to write one of my own before I got out of college.

Did I do it? No-o-o-o! I didn't need to because I thought I had everything under control. But I didn't, and I found myself at age thirty-nine asking the question, "What *is* important? What are my own SIMPLE RULES OF LIFE?" So twenty-two years after he told me about his list, I wrote one of my own. It also got narrowed down to six. To this day, I don't know if my rules are the same as Hal's, but I suspect they're similar. My list isn't in my wallet, but I look at it every day. And I promised myself that I'd try to live by these simple rules. Guess what. It worked! And it keeps on working.

You've read about each of the six in previous chapters, so there's nothing new here. This is just my way of reducing life to its bare essentials, the ones that can only be seen and understood with the heart.

WHAT'S ESSENTIAL

1. Choose a *good attitude,* no matter what the circumstances. Keep a positive outlook on life, and *always* be thankful.
2. Build your life on a foundation of *respect.* Love God, your family, and friends, and be kind to others. Bring ou' the best in everyone, including yourself.
3. Make integrity the cornerstone of your life. Follow the rules, play fair, and *be honest* in all things.

4. Accept the difficulties and challenges of life. **Work hard** at everything you do. And if you fail, try again.
5. Have a passion to **learn.** The more you discover about life and the world, the more complete and fulfilled you'll become. Make it a lifelong process.
6. Enjoy life. Remember that you need to play and have fun. And most of all, you need to **laugh.**

One cannot participate in this mysterious act of living with any hope of satisfaction unless one understands a few simple rules.

OG MANDINO

CHAPTER 20

Essential #1 Is Being a Good Person

Do all the good you can, by all the means you can.
JOHN WESLEY

A SIMPLE REASON FOR BEING GOOD

When I was a little kid, my behavior always seemed to improve right after Thanksgiving. The Christmas season had arrived, and we were told in some subtle and some not-so-subtle ways that there were rewards for being good. A familiar song reminded us over and over that Santa Claus was coming, and that we'd better watch out because he knew everything about us. He even knew whether we were sleeping or awake. But more important, he knew if we were being good or bad. That was serious stuff.

We had to be good if we were going to make a big haul on Christmas morning.

During the rest of the year, we were given two other reasons for being good. One of them was fear of punishment. If we messed up, we were going to pay for it, either by being denied a favorite activity or by getting the tar whaled out of us. Sometimes both. The other reason for being good was simply that we *should* be. We were told to obey the rules, be polite, and show respect for the rights and property of others. We weren't given a choice, and it wasn't even debatable. We were just supposed to be good.

Are the reasons for being good any different today? We can get rewarded for doing good things, whether it's at Christmas or not; we can get punished for doing bad things, and there are plenty of reminders around that we're *supposed* to be good. So external rewards, fear of punishment, and a sense of duty are still valid reasons for being good. But they're not the only ones. There's another reason that's much more basic and far more important.

BEING GOOD IS THE MOST ESSENTIAL INGREDIENT OF EMOTIONAL AND SPIRITUAL HEALTH

As human beings, we need to be good. That might seem so simple and obvious that you're wondering why I would conclude the book with it. But one of the most common mistakes we make is to overlook life's simplest and greatest truths. I did that for many years. It took me a long time to see one of the simplest truths of all: that there's a relationship between old-fashioned goodness and our health and well-being. Sadly, too many people never see it. I hope you do. And I hope with all my heart that this book helps, because old-fashioned goodness is the essence of every page in it.

What do I mean by old-fashioned goodness? I mean living by the great moral values that have been with us since God created the world. These time-honored values are the precious guidelines that bring order and give meaning to our lives. And they help us become the type of persons we were meant to be. Living right morally is the only way we can live peacefully with others and ourselves. That's why essential #1 is being a good person.

Only a life of goodness and honesty leaves us feeling spiritually healthy and human.

HAROLD KUSHNER

Conclusion

Almost two thousand years ago, St. Paul wrote a letter to his friends in Philippi. He said he prayed that they would have a love that was full of knowledge and insight. Then he added, "I want you to be able always to recognize the highest and the best. . . . I want to see your lives full of true goodness. . . ."

I hope this book has helped *you* recognize the highest and the best—in the world, in others, and in yourself. And my prayer for you is that your own life is full of true goodness.

A Few Books That Have Shaped My Thinking and My Life

How to Win Friends and Influence People by Dale Carnegie, New York: Simon & Schuster, 1936.

Mere Christianity by C. S. Lewis, New York: Macmillan, 1952.

No Man Is an Island by Thomas Merton, New York: Harcourt, Brace and Company, 1955.

The Art of Loving by Erich Fromm, New York: Harper, 1956.

Man's Search for Meaning by Viktor Frankl, New York: Pocket Books, 1959.

The Greatest Salesman in the World by Og Mandino, New York: Bantam, 1968.

The Confessions of Augustine in Modern English translated and abridged by Sherwood E. Wirt, Grand Rapids: Zondervan, 1971.

Your Erroneous Zones by Wayne W. Dyer, New York: Avon, 1976.

The Road Less Traveled by M. Scott Peck, New York: Simon & Schuster, 1978.

A Few Books That Have Shaped My Thinking

See You at the Top by Zig Ziglar, Gretna: Pelican Publishing, 1979.

You Gotta Keep Dancin' by Tim Hansel, Elgin, Ill.: D. C. Cook, 1985.

When All You Ever Wanted Isn't Enough by Harold S. Kushner, New York: Summit Books, 1986.

To Thine Own Self Be True by Lewis M. Andrews, Garden City: Anchor Press, 1987.

The 7 Habits of Highly Effective People by Stephen R. Covey, New York: Simon & Schuster, 1989.

First Things First by Stephen R. Covey, New York: Simon & Schuster, 1994.

Tuesdays with Morrie by Mitch Albom, New York: Doubleday, 1997.

The Gift of Peace by Joseph Cardinal Bernardin, Chicago: Loyola Press, 1997.

Wisdom of the Ages by Wayne W. Dyer, New York: Harper-Collins, 1998.

What Matters Most by Hyrum W. Smith, New York: Simon & Schuster, 2000.

The Old Testament, New International Version.

The New Testament, J. B. Phillips translation.

Thank You

One person can write a book, but it takes many insightful and caring people to breathe life into it, to give it meaning, and to spread its message. I've been richly blessed by these kinds of people in recent years, and I'm deeply grateful for the ways in which they've contributed to the success of the book and to the enrichment of my life.

Ruth Urban—Thank you, Mom, for planting the seeds from which this book has grown. You were both my first teacher and my best one. So many of the great lessons I've been passing on to others came originally from you. I learned them, not from what you said, but from what you did. Thank you for the lessons and for the way you taught them—gently, humbly, and with unconditional love.

Cathy Urban—Thank you for the love and support I've been able to count on since writing the first page. You've been everything an author needs: a gentle critic and editor, a trusted advisor, a source of great encouragement, and when needed, a sympathetic listener. Most important, you've been the best friend I've ever had.

Tom Lickona—Thank you for your incredible devotion to the cause of character education, and for so generously sharing your enthusiasm for the book. You've touched the lives of more kids, teachers, and parents than you'll ever know, and you've touched my life in a way that can't be described.

Tim Hansel—Thank you for being one of those rare persons who always looks for something good, and for teaching me to do the same. You've enhanced the quality of my life, and in turn, the content of this book. A great teacher's influence lasts forever.

Russ Sands—Thank you for being the kind of friend everyone needs—one who's always there with either good advice or a good laugh. Thanks for believing in the book and for continuing to share its message with others.

Mike Murray—Thank you for being the first person from the corporate world to urge me to take the book to a wider audience. Words can often have great impact, and what you wrote in your letter in the spring of 1996 changed my thinking. You inspired me to see new possibilities, and you've helped turn them into realities. Thanks for always being there with a fresh idea, and for tirelessly sharing my message with others.

Joe Durepos—Thank you for being so much more than a literary agent. It was my good fortune that you came along when I was in need of someone with both extensive knowledge and experience in the book industry. You have those, but what sealed the deal was your insight, warmth, integrity, and sense of humor. I'm honored to have you as my agent and equally honored to have you as my friend.

Caroline Sutton and Chris Lloreda—Thank you for proving that an editor and an associate publisher at a big New York publishing house can be absolutely delightful to work with. I've thoroughly enjoyed our relationship from the beginning, and deeply appreciate your professionalism, ethics, and accessibility. Thanks for your genuine enthusiasm for the book, for helping me improve upon it, and for making it possible to place these great lessons on a much larger stage. I'm happy and grateful to be on the same team with both of you.

Since the first edition of the book came out in 1992, I've been further blessed with a large number and a wide variety of new friends who've been determined to help spread my message. These wonderful people include educators, students, businessmen and -women, law-enforcement officers, a few prisoners, lawyers, family therapists, journalists, people in ministry, and private citizens. The list has grown so long, I can't possibly include all of your names here, but I do want to extend my heartfelt thanks. I know you want to make the world a better place, and I'm honored to be a part of your effort.

About the Author

Hal Urban holds bachelor's and master's degrees in history, and a doctorate in education and psychology from the University of San Francisco. He has also done postdoctoral work at Stanford University in the psychology of peak performance.

He is a man with a passion for teaching and a great love for young people. For thirty-five years, he devoted himself to bringing out the best in them, which included the three sons he raised as a single father, his students at San Carlos High School, Woodside High School, and the University of San Francisco.

Since the original version of the book was published in 1992, Dr. Urban has spoken throughout the world on positive character traits and their relationship to the quality of life. He makes presentations at national conventions, conducts workshops with educators, and speaks to students, parents, church groups, and people in business.

Information about his lectures and workshops can be obtained by viewing his website:

www.halurban.com

or by writing to him at

P.O. Box 5407
Redwood City, CA 94063

or call him at 650-366-0882.